Rails: Up and Running

Other resources from O'Reilly

Related titles
Advanced Rails

Ajax on Rails

Enterprise Rails

Rails Cookbook™

Rails Pocket Reference

Ruby Cookbook™

The Ruby Programming
   Language

oreilly.com
oreilly.com is more than a complete catalog of O'Reilly books. You'll also find links to news, events, articles, weblogs, sample chapters, and code examples.

oreillynet.com is the essential portal for developers interested in open and emerging technologies, including new platforms, programming languages, and operating systems.

Conferences
O'Reilly brings diverse innovators together to nurture the ideas that spark revolutionary industries. We specialize in documenting the latest tools and systems, translating the innovator's knowledge into useful skills for those in the trenches. Visit *conferences.oreilly.com* for our upcoming events.

Safari Bookshelf (*safari.oreilly.com*) is the premier online reference library for programmers and IT professionals. Conduct searches across more than 1,000 books. Subscribers can zero in on answers to time-critical questions in a matter of seconds. Read the books on your Bookshelf from cover to cover or simply flip to the page you need. Try it today for free.

SECOND EDITION

Rails: Up and Running

Bruce A. Tate, Lance Carlson, and Curt Hibbs

O'REILLY®

Beijing · Cambridge · Farnham · Köln · Sebastopol · Taipei · Tokyo

Rails: Up and Running, Second Edition

by Bruce A. Tate, Lance Carlson, and Curt Hibbs

Published by O'Reilly Media, Inc., 1005 Gravenstein Highway North, Sebastopol, CA 95472.

O'Reilly books may be purchased for educational, business, or sales promotional use. Online editions are also available for most titles (*http://safari.oreilly.com*). For more information, contact our corporate/institutional sales department: (800) 998-9938 or *corporate@oreilly.com*.

Editor: Mike Loukides		**Indexer:** Fred Brown	
Production Editor: Sumita Mukherji		**Cover Designer:** Karen Montgomery	
Copyeditor: Sumita Mukherji		**Interior Designer:** David Futato	
Proofreader: Sada Preisch		**Illustrator:** Robert Romano	

Printing History:

August 2006:	First Edition.
October 2008:	Second Edition.

ISBN: 978-0-596-52200-1

[M]

1222436893

Table of Contents

Preface

The Rails phenomenon is sweeping through our industry with reckless disregard for established programming languages, long-standing conventions, or commercial support. You can get a whole lot of information about Rails from articles on the Web, excellent books, and even formal course work. However, there's something missing: how does an established programmer—armed with nothing more than a little Ruby knowledge—go just beyond the basics and be productive in Rails?

With *Rails: Up and Running*, Second Edition, we are not going to reiterate the reference manual or replace Google. Instead, we'll strive to give you the big picture of how Rails applications hold together and tell you where to go for the information that we don't cover in the chapters. We'll take you just beneath the covers of Active Record, the Rails framework that gives Ruby objects a database backing. You'll get just deep enough to understand the "magic" features that perplex most Rails newbies. By understanding the big picture, you'll be able to make better use of the best reference manuals to fill in the details.

We won't try to make you digest a whole lot of words. Rather, we'll give you the theory in the context of an end-to-end application. We'll walk you through the creation of a simple project—one that is a little more demanding than a blog or shopping cart, but with a simple enough structure that a Rails beginner will be able to quickly understand what's going on. In short, we're going to let the code do the talking, and we'll augment that code where you'll need some help to understand exactly what's going on.

We're not going to try to cover each new feature. Instead, we'll show you the ones we see as the backbone, forming the most important elements to understand. We will also cover the new migrations and REST features in some detail because various older books don't cover those features in too much detail.

In short, we're not trying to build a comprehensive Rails library—we're going to give you the foundation you need to get up and running.

Who Should Read This Book?

Rails: Up and Running, Second Edition, is for experienced developers who are new to Rails and possibly to Ruby. To use this book, you don't have to be a strong Ruby programmer; we do expect you to be a programmer, though. You should know enough about your chosen platform to be able to write programs, install software, run scripts using the system console, edit files, use a database, and understand how basic web applications work.

Conventions Used in This Book

The following typographic conventions are used in this book:

Plain text
> Indicates menu titles, menu options, menu buttons, and keyboard accelerators (such as Alt and Ctrl).

Italic
> Indicates emphasis, new terms, URLs, email addresses, filenames, file extensions, pathnames, directories, and Unix utilities.

`Constant width`
> Indicates commands, the contents of files, and the output from commands.

`Constant width bold`
> Shows commands or other text that should be typed literally by the user.

`Constant width italic`
> Shows text that should be replaced with user-supplied values.

> This icon signifies a tip, suggestion, or general note.

> This icon indicates a warning or caution.

Using Code Examples

This book is here to help you get your job done. In general, you may use the code in this book in your programs and documentation. You do not need to contact us for permission unless you're reproducing a significant portion of the code. For example, writing a program that uses several chunks of code from this book does not require permission. Selling or distributing a CD-ROM of examples from O'Reilly books *does* require permission. Answering a question by citing this book and quoting example code does not require permission. Incorporating a significant amount of example code from this book into your product's documentation *does* require permission.

You can get sample code at the main page for *Rails: Up and Running*, Second Edition: *http://www.oreilly.com/catalog/9780596522001*. You will find a ZIP file that contains the sample project as it exists after each chapter, with each instance of the sample application numbered by chapter. If you want to skip a chapter, just download the right ZIP file.

We appreciate, but do not require, attribution. An attribution usually includes the title, author, publisher, and ISBN. For example: "*Rails: Up and Running* by Bruce A. Tate, Curt Hibbs, and Lance Carlson. Copyright 2009 Bruce A. Tate, Lance Carlson, and Curt Hibbs, 978-0-596-52200-1."

If you feel that your use of code examples falls outside fair use or the permission given here, feel free to contact us at *permissions@oreilly.com*.

Platforms

Rails is cross-platform, but Unix and Windows shells behave differently. For consistency, we use Mac OS X version 10.5.2 throughout this book. You can easily run the examples on the Unix or Windows operating systems as well. You'll see a few minor differences:

- You can specify paths with the forward slash (/) or backslash (\) character on Windows. We'll try to be consistent and use the forward slash to specify all paths.

- To run the various Ruby scripts that make up Rails on Windows, you need to explicitly type `ruby`. On Unix environments, you don't. We will remind you a few times early in the book. If you're running Unix, and you are instructed to type the command `ruby script/server`, feel free to omit the `ruby`.

- To run a process in a separate shell on Windows, precede the command with `start`. On Unix and Mac OS X, append an ampersand (&) character to run the command in the background.

Safari® Books Online

Safari _{Books Online}   When you see a Safari® Books Online icon on the cover of your favorite technology book, that means the book is available online through the O'Reilly Network Safari Bookshelf.

Safari offers a solution that's better than e-books. It's a virtual library that lets you easily search thousands of top tech books, cut and paste code samples, download chapters, and find quick answers when you need the most accurate, current information. Try it for free at *http://safari.oreilly.com*.

How to Contact Us

We have tested and verified the information in this book and in the source code to the best of our ability, but given the amount of text and the rapid evolution of technology, you may find that features have changed or that we have made mistakes. If so, please notify us by writing to:

O'Reilly Media, Inc.
1005 Gravenstein Highway North
Sebastopol, CA 95472
800-998-9938 (in the United States or Canada)
707-829-0515 (international or local)
707-829-0104 (fax)

You can also send messages electronically. To be put on the mailing list or request a catalog, send email to:

info@oreilly.com

To ask technical questions or comment on the book, send email to:

bookquestions@oreilly.com

As mentioned in the earlier section, we have a website for this book where you can find code, errata (previously reported errors and corrections available for public view), and other book information. You can access this website at:

http://www.oreilly.com/catalog/9780596522001

For more information about this book and others, see the O'Reilly website:

http://www.oreilly.com

Acknowledgments

Writing a book is a demanding exercise, taking passion, commitment, and persistence. The authors on the cover get all of the glory (and possibly the blame). Many people contribute to a book. We'd like to mention the people who made writing this book such a fulfilling experience.

Collectively, Bruce, Lance, and Curt would like to thank the outstanding team of reviewers who provided so many great comments, including David Mabelle, Mauro Cicio, Brooke Hedrick, Faisal Jawdat, Shane Claussen, Leo de Blaauw, Anne Bowman, Seth Havermann, Dave Hastings, and Randy Hanford. We'd also like to thank David Geary for fleshing out some of the early ideas in Photo Share.

Rails: Up and Running, Second Edition, would be nothing without the excellent contributions of the core Rails team. We would like to thank David Heinemeier Hansson (the creator of Rails), Florian Weber, Jamis Buck, Jeremy Kemper, Leon Breedt, Marcel

Molina Jr., Michael Koziarski, Nicholas Seckar, Sam Stephenson, Scott Barron, Thomas Fuchs, and Tobias Luetke. Ruby is a fantastic language, and we would like to thank the many who made it so. We throw out specific thanks to Yukihiro Matsumoto (a.k.a. "Matz"), the creator of Ruby, and to Dave Thomas and Andy Hunt, without whom Ruby might have remained virtually unknown outside of Japan.

Bruce would like to specifically thank Curt for stepping into this project after it seemed that it was dead. Also, thanks to those at AutoGas who were so instrumental in trying this technology within the context of a real production application—especially the core development team, including Mathew Varghese, Karl Hoenshel, Cheri Byerley, Chris Gindorf, and Colby Blaisdell. Their collective experience shaped this book more than you will ever know. Thanks to my Dutch friend Leo, again, for being such a supportive influence on this book, though you're mostly a Java™ developer. You have had more influence on me than you might expect. More than anyone else, I would like to thank my family. Kayla and Julia, you are the sparks in my soul that keep the creative fires burning. Maggie, you are my inspiration, and I love you more than I can ever say.

Lance would like to thank Bruce Tate for giving him the opportunity to help write the second edition of this book. I would also like to personally thank the rails core team and Matz for ending his PHP career. Also, I'd like to thank Wayne Seguin who was the best boss ever. Thanks goes to all of those I worked with at Engine Yard for seeing my potential despite my age. Respect and thanks go to Joe O'Brien, Jim Weirich and Stuart Halloway for emphasizing TDD and bringing me to enlightenment. Last, but not least, I'd like to thank my girlfriend Alison who stuck with me when I wasn't making any money and made me realize my true value as a web developer and entrepreneur.

Curt would like to thank his wife, Wasana, for letting him disappear behind his computer screen late into the night (and sometimes into the following day) without complaint. I would also like to thank my friends at O'Reilly for giving me a forum to spread the word about the incredible productivity advantages of Rails. Specifically, I'd like to thank chromatic for publishing my ONLamp.com articles, and Mike Loukides for not giving up when I kept telling him I didn't want to write a book.

## CHAPTER 1

Zero to Sixty: Introducing Rails

When we wrote the first version of this book, Rails was just starting to ramp up as a framework. Now, the exploding web development platform is working its way into the mainstream. Companies like Twitter have bet on Rails and won big, and others have tried Rails and crashed hard. You should be comfortable that you're entering this ecosystem not as a pioneer, but as part of a much greater wave that's sweeping through the whole computing profession. If you read the first edition, you'll notice that we're not selling the framework quite so hard. In all honesty, we don't have to. Let's lay the basic foundation so we can get to work.

Rails is a framework for building database-backed web applications. Based on the Ruby programming language, Rails is best for applications that need to be developed quickly without sacrificing a clean structure that can also be well-maintained. Ruby is interpreted, but it's fast enough to attack websites with all but the most demanding performance characteristics. And it's tremendously popular. That popularity means you can find what you need to build projects in Rails.

Since the first edition of this book was released, the Rails core team released milestone versions 1.1, 1.2, 2.0, and now 2.1. Today, you can find excellent hosting from dozens of vendors depending on how much management you're willing to do. And technical officers like me (Bruce Tate) are bringing Rails into the enterprise to run our core businesses. The Rails framework has since led to rapid investment in the Ruby programming language, too, including evolving implementations on the Java Virtual Machine, the Microsoft Common Language Runtime, and two emerging Ruby virtual machines. Rails is also redefining web development frameworks in other languages as well. Java, PHP, Python, Lisp, Groovy, and Perl each have more than one Rails-like framework. The Rails convention-based approach is overtaking standard configuration-based approaches just about everywhere.

In this book, we will walk you through everything you need to get a simple application up and running. We promise to move slowly enough that you can absorb the concepts, but quickly enough so that you will have a working application after following along for a few hours. Let's get started.

Putting Rails into Action

We're going to blow through installation quickly because installation details can change with Rails itself and the individual platforms that support it. The best place to go, regardless of your platform, is the Rails wiki at *http://wiki.rubyonrails.org/rails/pa ges/GettingStartedWithRails*. We'll give you a condensed version here: you'll install Ruby, Rails, and then your database. First, install Ruby. If you're running OS X, chances are good that Ruby is already there, but older versions will need an upgrade. If you're running Windows, there are some good one-click installers that you can use such as the Ruby one-click installer at *http://rubyinstaller.rubyforge.org*. For now, just install Ruby, and we'll walk you through the rest.

Once you've installed Ruby, you could manually install all of the components for Rails, but Ruby has a packaging and deployment feature named *gems*. The gem installer accesses a central repository and downloads an application unit, called a gem, and all its dependencies. If you haven't done so, install Rails with this command:[*]

```
sudo gem install rails --include-dependencies  -v 2.1
```

The command for installing Ruby components on all platforms is the same: gem install. The permissions required will vary from platform to platform. On OS X, sudo elevates your permissions for this command to superuser status. You'll want to omit the sudo portion of this command on Windows. If things go well, you'll see a list of a bunch of different gems fly by. These are Rails and all of the dependencies that Rails requires. That's it—Rails is installed. There's one caveat: you also need to install the database support for your given database. In this book, we're going to use SQLite, but you can use any database engine supported by Rails. On Unix, chances are SQLite is already installed. On Windows, you'll need to pull down the SQLite DLL and command-line client. For more details, go to *http://wiki.rubyonrails.com/rails/pages/How toUseSQLite*. With Ruby, Rails, and a database, you're ready to create a project:

```
>rails chapter-1
      create
      create    app/controllers
      create    app/helpers
      create    app/models
      create    app/views/layouts
      create    config/environments
      create    components
      create    db
      create    doc
      create    lib

...

      create    test/functional
      create    test/integration
```

---

[*] If you want to code along with us, make sure you've installed Ruby and gems. Appendix A contains detailed installation instructions.

```
    create  test/unit
    create  vendor
...
    create  app/controllers/application.rb
    create  app/helpers/application_helper.rb
    create  test/test_helper.rb
    create  config/database.yml
...
```

MVC and Model2

In the mid-1970s, the MVC (model-view-controller) strategy evolved in the Smalltalk community to reduce coupling between business logic and presentation logic. With MVC, you put your business logic into separate domain objects and isolate your presentation logic in a view, which presents data from domain objects. The controller manages navigation between views, processes user input, and marshals the correct domain objects between the model and view. Good programmers have used MVC ever since, implementing MVC applications using frameworks written in many different languages, including Ruby.

Web developers use a subtly different variant as MVC called *Model2*. Model2 uses the same principles of MVC, but tailors them for stateless web applications. In Model2 applications, a browser calls a controller via web standards. The controller invokes the model layer to do business functions such as getting database data, and then makes model objects available to the view for display. Next, the controller calls the view layer, which renders a view. This view is typically a web page, but might also be an XML form or some other type of view. The framework then returns the web page to the user. In the Rails community, when someone says MVC, they're referring to the Model2 variant.

Model2 has been tremendously successful through the years. Many different frameworks across dozens of programming languages use it. In the Java community, Struts is the most common Model2 framework. In Python, the flagship web development frameworks called Zope and Django both use Model2. You can read more about the model-view-controller strategy at *http://en.wikipedia.org/wiki/Model-view-controller*.

We truncated the list, but you get the picture. Rails creates folders that you'll use to hold the model, view, and controller portions of your application code, different kinds of test cases, database configuration, and third-party libraries that you might choose to install later. All Rails projects will use this same organization with a few slight variations. You'll run just about all of your Rails scripts from your new project directory. Go to your project directory with `cd chapter-1`. In the next section, we'll take a look at the organization of your project in more detail.

Organization

The directories created during installation provide a place for your application code, scripts to help you manage and build your application, and many other goodies. Later, we'll examine the most interesting directories in greater detail. For now, let's take a quick pass through the directory tree in the project we created:

app
> This directory has your Rails application. You'll spend most of your development time working on files in this directory. *app* has subdirectories that hold the view (*views* and *helpers*), controller (*controllers*), and the backend business logic (*models*).

config
> This directory contains the small amount of configuration code that your application will need. Your database configuration will go in *database.yml*. Common environmental configuration, such as the configuration of any mail server your application needs, will go in *environment.rb*. Rules for your URLs that route incoming web requests go in *routes.rb*. You can also specifically tailor the behavior of the three Rails environments for test (*environments/test.rb*), development (*environments/development.rb*), and production (*environments/production.rb*) with files found in the *environments* directory.

db
> Your Rails application will have model objects that access relational database tables. Files that describe the schema (*schema.rb*) go in this directory. *Migrations*, Ruby scripts that make it easy to code changes in your database schema, go in the *db/migrations* directory.

doc
> Ruby has a framework, called *RubyDoc*, that can automatically generate documentation for code you create. You can assist *RubyDoc* with comments in your code. This directory holds all the *RubyDoc*-generated Rails and application documentation.

lib
> You'll put common Rails libraries here, unless they explicitly belong elsewhere (such as vendor libraries). For example, common authentication libraries might go in this directory.

log
> Error logs go here. Rails creates scripts that help you manage various error logs. You'll find separate logs for the server (*server.log*) and each Rails environment (*development.log*, *test.log*, and *production.log*).

public
> Like the *public* directory for a web server, this directory has web files that don't change, such as JavaScript files (*public/javascripts*), graphics (*public/images*), stylesheets (*public/stylesheets*), and HTML files (*public*). Some Rails caching solutions also create *.html* files that go in the *public* directory.

script

This directory holds scripts to launch and manage the various tools that you'll use with Rails. For example, there are scripts to generate (*generate*) and delete (*destroy*) code and launch the web server (*server*). Other scripts launch a console (*console*) for managing your application and debugging or installing and removing plug-ins (*plugin*). You'll learn much more about using many of these scripts throughout this book.

test

The tests you write and those Rails creates for you all go here. You'll see a subdirectory for mocks (*mocks*), unit tests (*unit*), integration tests (*integration*), fixtures (*fixtures*), and functional tests (*functional*). We'll cover a brief introduction to testing in Chapter 7.

tmp

Rails uses this directory to hold temporary files for intermediate processing.

vendor

Libraries provided by third-party vendors (such as security libraries, plug-ins, or database utilities beyond the basic Rails distribution) go here.

Except for minor changes between releases, every Rails project will have the same structure, with the same naming conventions. This consistency gives you a tremendous advantage; you can quickly move between Rails projects without relearning the project's organization. The Rails framework itself also relies on this consistency because the different Rails frameworks will often discover files solely on naming conventions and directory structure.

The Web Server

Now that we've got a project, let's start the web server. If you haven't already done so, type **cd chapter-1** to switch to your project directory. Use the *script/server* script to start an instance of the Mongrel server configured for development. If you're running Windows, each time you see a command that's prefaced with the script directory, preface the call instead with **ruby**, using forward or backward slashes. If you're using most other platforms, you can omit the **ruby** keyword. From here on out, we'll skip the **ruby** part of the command. Type **script/server** now:

```
$ script/server

=> Booting Mongrel (use 'script/server webrick' to force WEBrick)
=> Rails application starting on http://0.0.0.0:3000
=> Call with -d to detach
=> Ctrl-C to shutdown server
** Starting Mongrel listening at 0.0.0.0:3000
** Starting Rails with development environment...
** Rails loaded.
** Loading any Rails specific GemPlugins
** Signals ready.  TERM => stop.  USR2 => restart.  INT => stop (no restart).
```

```
** Rails signals registered.  HUP => reload (without restart).  It might not work well.
** Mongrel 1.1.1 available at 0.0.0.0:3000
** Use CTRL-C to stop.
```

Notice these details:

- The server started on port 3000. You can change the port number and other startup details with command-line options. See the sidebar "Configuring the Server" for more configuration options.

- We started an instance of Mongrel, the default web server. You can configure Rails to start many kinds of web servers.

- Ruby will also let you use a backward slash as a path delimiter on the command line, but on Unix, you must use the forward slash. Some prefer the backslash on Windows because it allows you to use the tab completion feature in the MS-DOS command prompt.

Configuring the Server

If you need to, you can configure the port, the directory for public files, and other server features with command-line options. You can see the options by adding the --help switch. Here are the default options for Rails 2.0:

```
> script/server --help
=> Booting Mongrel (use 'script/server webrick' to force WEBrick)
Usage: server [options]
    -p, --port=port                  Runs Rails on the specified port.
                                     Default: 3000
    -b, --binding=ip                 Binds Rails to the specified ip.
                                     Default: 0.0.0.0
    -d, --daemon                     Make server run as a Daemon.
    -u, --debugger                   Enable ruby-debugging for the server.
    -e, --environment=name           Specifies the environment to run this server
                                     under (test/development/production).
                                     Default: development

    -h, --help                       Show this help message.
```

You won't need to customize this script directly. The command-line switches should give you everything you need.

Point your browser to *http://localhost:3000/*. You'll see the Rails welcome screen pictured in Figure 1-1. Don't worry about the details of the request yet; for now, know that Rails is running and working correctly.

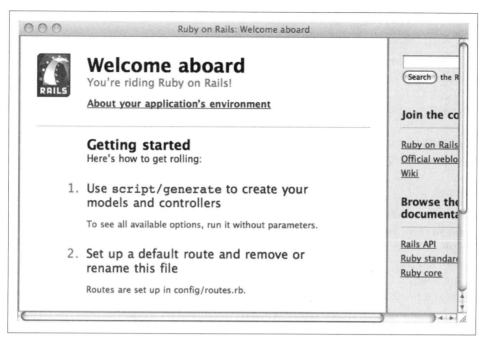

Figure 1-1. The Rails welcome screen

So far, you've already set up the build environment, typed a few words, and verified that the server is running. In the development environment, you'll normally leave the server up, rebooting only to make major configuration changes for things such as new gems or a changed database configuration.

Choosing a Server

Rails will run on many different web servers. Most of your development will be done using Mongrel, but you'll probably want to run production code on one of the alternative servers. Let's look briefly at the available servers.

Apache

Although WEBrick is the most convenient choice, it's not the most scalable or flexible. The Apache web server is the most widely deployed web server in the world. You can choose from an incredible array of plug-ins to run dozens of programming languages or serve other kinds of dynamic content. Apache scales well, with outstanding caching plug-ins and good support for load balancers (machines that efficiently spread requests across multiple web servers). If you're looking for a safe solution, look no further than the Apache web server.

nginx

Apache is a good general-purpose web server, but it's not the most specialized one. nginx has replaced lighttpd in the Rails community as the lightweight web server that's built for one thing: speed. It serves static content such as HTML web pages and images very quickly, and it supports applications through Mongrel and Mongrel Cluster. nginx does not have nearly as many flexible plug-ins or the marketing clout of the Apache web server, but if you're looking for a specialized server to serve static content and Rails applications quickly, nginx could be your answer. It's fairly young, but it has a great reputation for speed among Rails enthusiasts.

Mongrel

Although Apache and lighttpd are very fast and scalable production servers, configuring them to serve your Rails application can sometimes be challenging, and it is never as simple as WEBrick. Mongrel changes all of that. Mongrel combines the advantages of WEBrick (because it's written in Ruby) and nginx (because it's written for speed and clusters well). This combination could make Mongrel an excellent choice for development and production. You can quickly cluster Mongrel with MongrelCluster. Be careful, though—Mongrel does not serve static content very quickly. For demanding deployments, you'll want to combine Mongrel with one of the web servers mentioned above, likely Apache or nginx.

WEBrick

WEBrick, once the default development server for Rails, is written entirely in Ruby. It supports the standards you'll need—HTTP for communications, HTML for web pages, and ERb for embedding Ruby code into web pages for dynamic content. WEBrick is generally not used anymore, even in pure development mode. Mongrel has taken its place.

Other web servers

Theoretically, any web server that supports CGI can serve a Rails application. Unfortunately, CGI with Rails is dead slow, so it is really not suitable for production. However, if you are running in a specialized environment that has its own web server, you can probably get it to serve your Rails application using the FastCGI or SCGI interfaces. Do a web search first, because it's very likely that someone else has already done it and posted instructions. For example, if you must deploy your Rails application on Microsoft's IIS, you will find that many developers have done this already. You'll probably see other web servers rapidly move to support Rails. You can also find plenty of information on lighttpd with FastCGI. Deploying Rails applications is far beyond the scope of this book.

Now that your server is up, it's time to write some code. We'll focus on simple controllers and views in the rest of this chapter.

Creating a Controller

You've seen that Rails organizes applications into pieces with a model, view, and controller. We'll start with the controller. Use the *generate* script to create a controller. In Chapter 2, we'll talk more about the generator for controllers. For now, we'll specify the type of object to create first and then the name of the new controller. Type:

```
$ ruby script/generate controller greeting
      exists  app/controllers/
      exists  app/helpers/
      create  app/views/greeting
      exists  test/functional/
      create  app/controllers/greeting_controller.rb
      create  test/functional/greeting_controller_test.rb
      create  app/helpers/greeting_helper.rb
```

You might not have expected to see so much activity. Rails created your expected controller: *greeting_controller.rb*. But you also got a few other files as well:

application.rb

There is not yet a controller for the whole application, so Rails created this one. It will come in handy later as a place to anchor application-wide concerns, such as security.

views/greeting

Rails knows that controllers render views, so it created a directory called *views/ greeting*.

greeting_controller_test.rb

Rails also created a test for your new controller because most Rails developers build automated unit tests to make it easy to build in and maintain quality.

greeting_helper.rb

Rails helpers provide a convenient place to set repetitive or complicated code that might otherwise reside in your views. By separating this code, you can keep your views clean and simple.

Rails creators built the framework to first solve their own problems. As a result, you see plenty of practical experience in the framework. The generators are a great example of that practical experience in action. You get a combination of all the application files that you'll need to build the controller.

Mapping params

Let's discuss what has happened so far. When the web server calls Rails, the router matches a URL to the route. Before invoking a controller, Rails builds a hash of par ams based on the chosen route. The router also adds any additional URL parameters to the params hash. You can easily see what's in the params hash by directly rendering some text. Add the following code to *app/controllers/greeting_controller.rb* to see the params:

```
class GreetingController < ApplicationController

  def index
  end

  def show
    render :text => params.inspect
  end
end
```

Now, point your browser to *http://localhost:3000/greeting/show*. You should see the text {"action"=>"show", "controller"=>"greeting"}. The Rails router set the action and controller keys. Try a more complicated URL, as shown in Example 1-1.

Example 1-1. Rails builds a hash from a URL

```
For URL: http://localhost:3000/greeting/show/1?key=value&another_key=value
The hash is: {"action"=>"show",
             "id"=>"1",
             "controller"=>"greeting",
             "another_key"=>"value",
             "key"=>"value"}
```

Much of the time, in Rails, you're dealing with URLs that amount to nothing more than a bunch of key/value pairs. On the URL, these are query strings. In Ruby, they're a hash. Don't let these hashes be a mystery. The routes table found in *config/routes.rb* will tell you exactly how Rails will carve the URL into a convenient list of parameters. You'll see much more in the next chapter, but for now, it's time to build a view.

Building a View

You now have a controller that renders text, but this design can take you only so far. Ideally, you'd like to separate the HTML in the view from your business logic in your controllers and models. The sloppy design is easy enough to fix. If you want to follow Rails MVC conventions, you should render text in a separate view instead of from your controller. Instead of the render command in the greeting controller, you can render the text in a Rails view. As with many web frameworks, Rails can use a template strategy for the view. A template is simply an HTML page with Ruby code mixed in. A Ruby engine called *ERb* interprets the template on the server, adding dynamic content to your page. That page will usually be written in HTML, but you can design templates for XML pages or email, too.

Figure 1-2. Rails documentation for the controller

Documentation

Unlike many open source (*http://opensource.org*) projects, Rails has excellent documentation. You can find it all at *http://api.rubyonrails.com*. You'll find overviews, tutorials, and even movies. You can always find the API document for the latest version of Rails at the site, with a full set of documents for every class in the Rails API. You can also find it with your Rails installation.

The excellent Rails documentation is not an accident. Like Java, Ruby comes with a utility called RubyDoc that generates documentation from source code and comments that you provide within the source code. When you install Ruby Gems, it also installs the documentation for the gem. Figure 1-2 shows the documentation for a controller.

With Rails, you can generate an empty view and some helpers that the view will need along with your controller. Type the `script/destroy controller greeting` command to destroy the previous controller:

```
$ ruby script/destroy controller greeting

      rm   app/helpers/greeting_helper.rb
      rm   test/functional/greeting_controller_test.rb
      rm   app/controllers/greeting_controller.rb
   rmdir   test/functional
```

```
notempty  test
   rmdir  app/views/greeting
notempty  app/views
notempty  app
notempty  app/helpers
notempty  app
notempty  app/controllers
notempty  app
```

Next, type `script/generate controller greeting index` to generate a controller with the index action and index view:

```
$ ruby script/generate controller greeting index

exists  app/controllers/
exists  app/helpers/
create  app/views/greeting
create  test/functional/
create  app/controllers/greeting_controller.rb
create  test/functional/greeting_controller_test.rb
create  app/helpers/greeting_helper.rb
create  app/views/greeting/index.html.erb
```

See also Figure 1-3.

Figure 1-3. Rails documentation for the controller

The generator created the view, *index.html.erb*, with helper and test files. From the output, you can see that the generator created a few directories, a controller called `greeting_controller.rb`, a helper called `greeting_helper.rb`, and a test called `greeting_controller_test.rb`. Take a look at the new `index` method in controller, called `app/controllers/greeting_controller.rb`:

```
class GreetingController < ApplicationController

    def index
    end
end
```

This controller example uses *Action Pack*, the Rails framework responsible for implementing the view and controller parts of Rails. Unlike most MVC frameworks, your `index` method *didn't* specify a view. If your controller doesn't explicitly call **render**, Rails uses naming conventions to decide which view to render. The controller's name determines the view's directory, and the action name determines the name of the view. An action is a method on a controller. In this case, Action Pack fires the view in *app/views/greeting/index.html.erb*. You didn't have to edit any XML files or type any additional code to wire the controller to the view. You just allowed Rails to provide consistent naming conventions and infer your intent from there.

Now, edit the view. You'll find this data:

```
<h1>Greeting#index</h1>
<p>Find me in app/views/greeting/index.html.erb</p>
```

Point your browser to *http://localhost:3000/greetings/index* to see the previous message in HTML. Rails tells you where to find the file, should you ever render an unimplemented view. This empty file awaits an implementation.

Tying Controller Data to the View

In MVC, the view needs to render any data the controller provides. That data may come from model logic, the session, or any other source. Regardless of where the data comes from, in Rails, instance variables in the controller are available to the view. Let's try setting a variable called `@welcome_message` in the controller:

```
class GreetingController < ApplicationController
  def index
    @welcome_message = "Welcome to your first Rails application"
  end
end
```

Now, display the new message in the view by adding a Ruby expression between the `<%=` and `%>` tags. Rails renders the value of the expression within these tags, just as if the value of the expression had been printed in place. Here's a view that prints your welcome message as a level one heading:

```
<h1><%= @welcome_message %></h1>
```

Reload. You'll see the output from the view, with the message you created in the `index` method. In Example 1-1, you rendered your view within the controller. Here, you built an *HTML.ERB template*. Your HTML tags provided static structure and style, and your Ruby code provided dynamic content—in this case, a variable set within the controller. That's MVC.

Expressions and Scriptlets

When you're embedding Ruby code within a view template, you've got two options. *Scriptlets* are Ruby code placed between the `<%` and `%>` tags. Scriptlets run Ruby code without printing the results. You will often use a scriptlet to loop through the elements of a Ruby array, for example. *Expressions* are Ruby expressions placed between the `<%=` and `%>` tags. An expression presents the *value* returned by the Ruby code. You will use an expression to place the result of any Ruby code in a web page, just as if you'd printed the code there.

You can experiment with the interaction between the controller and view. We've changed the controller and view for greeting to show a few examples of expressions and scriptlets in action. First, we'll set a few values in the controller:

```
class GreetingController < ApplicationController
  def index
    @age=8
    @table={"headings" => ["addend", "addend", "sum"],
            "body"     => [[1, 1, 2], [1, 2, 3], [ 1, 3, 4]]
           }
  end
end
```

Next, here's the views/index.html.erb view showing expressions and scriptlets, both of which interact with values set in the controller:

```
<h1>Simple expression</h1>
<p>Tommy is <%= @age %> years old.</p>
```

Now, display the value of the instance variable @age, which was set in the controller:

```
<h1>Iteration using scriptlets</h1>
<% for i in 1..5 %>
  <p>Heading number <%= i %> </p>
<% end %>
```

Iterate with a scriptlet and show the current count with an expression:

```
<h1>A simple table</h1>

<table>
  <tr>
    <% @table["headings"].each do |head| %>
      <td>
        <b><%= head %></b>
      </td>
    <% end %>
  </tr>

  <% @table["body"].each do |row| %>
    <tr>
      <% row.each do |col| %>
        <td>
          <%= col %>
        </td>
      <% end %>
    </tr>
  <% end %>

</table>
```

Finally, use both techniques to display the contents of `@table`.

You'll get the results shown in Figure 1-4.

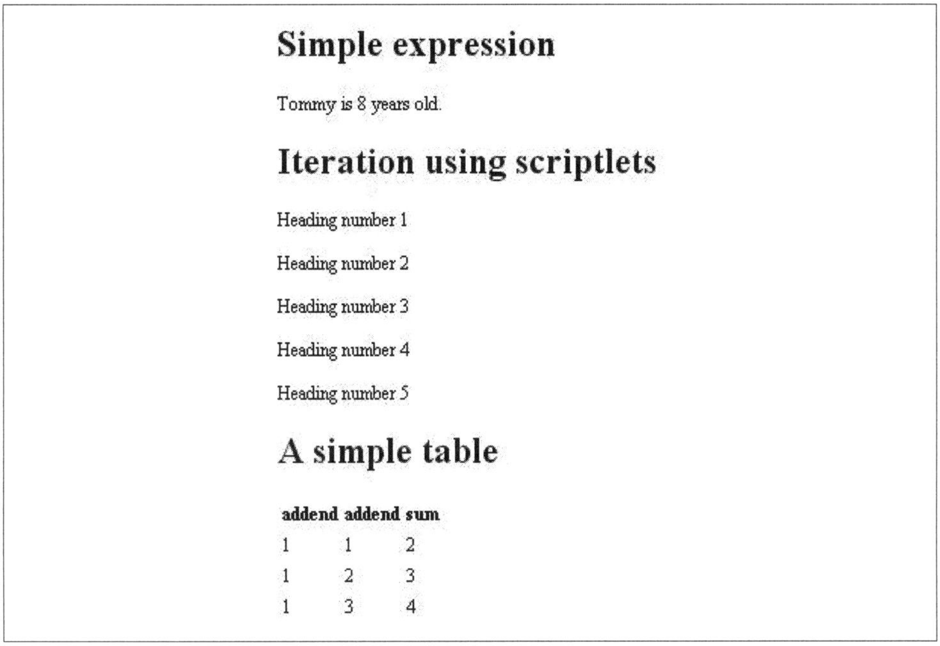

Simple expression

Tommy is 8 years old.

Iteration using scriptlets

Heading number 1

Heading number 2

Heading number 3

Heading number 4

Heading number 5

A simple table

addend	addend	sum
1	1	2
1	2	3
1	3	4

Figure 1-4. Results of embedded scriptlets and expressions

Under the Hood

As shown earlier, each time you submit a URL, you're creating an HTTP request, which fires a controller action. Any MVC framework designer needs to decide between reusing the same controller for each request and creating a new controller copy per request. Rails uses the latter strategy, which it calls *request scope*. Each HTTP request results in a new controller instance, meaning that you'll also get a new set of instance variables for each HTTP request. That's going to affect you in at least two different ways:

- On the plus side, you don't need to worry about threading in your controllers because each request gets a private copy of the controller's instance data.
- On the minus side, it will be harder for you to share instance data between requests, and Rails will take more resources. Specifically, if you set instance variables in one controller action method, don't expect to be able to use them in later HTTP requests, even if you simply redirect your request. You'll need to share them in a session, a cookie, or the URL.

What's Next?

You've created a Rails project. You've created a controller and invoked it from a browser. You've also created a view and learned how views can interact with controllers and with the Ruby language. The next chapter will show you a more extensive look at views and controllers. You'll use what you know, and some new tricks, to scaffold together a pretty sophisticated application that you'll use as the foundation for the rest of the book. Let's code.

## CHAPTER 2

Scaffolding, REST, and Routes

For centuries, scaffolding has helped builders provide access and support to buildings through the early stages of the construction process. Programmers, too, use temporary scaffolding code to lend structure and support until more permanent code is available. Rails automates scaffolding to make early coding more productive than ever before.

In Chapter 1, you saw how Rails took the most basic Rails request to call an action on a controller with a hash map of parameters. You also built some primitive views. In this chapter, we'll start building a more powerful application called Photo Share, one that you can use to manage your personal photographs. We'll use scaffolding to build the basic template, which includes a database-backed model, a controller, and a view. Along the way, you'll learn the basics of a few critical Rails features, including:

- *Migrations.* This database feature helps database developers create a database schema in steps, managing differences in the schema across all of your environments. Migrations will use Ruby code instead of database-specific SQL code.

- *REST and resources.* Rails leans heavily on a style of Internet communication called *REST*, or Representational State Transfer. This HTTP-based communication strategy defines Internet resources where each URL or HTTP command of any kind will do a CRUD operation (Create, Read, Update, or Delete) on that resource. In Rails 2, each controller is a REST resource.

- *Named routes.* For each resource, Rails creates named routes that map standardized, pretty URLs onto predetermined controller actions. The result for you is less programming, and better consistency across your application.

Let's take a closer look at the Photo Share application. Then, we'll quickly build out a basic application. By the time you complete this chapter, you'll have a primitive application that will manage photos, slideshows, slides, and categories.

Introducing Photo Share

For the remainder of this book, we'll be working on a single application called Photo Share, a database-backed web application that allows users to share photos among acquaintances. We'll start with these simple requirements, called *user stories*:

- View a set of photos on the Web so others can see them.
- Organize photos in categories.
- Organize and view slideshows from available photos.

These requirements each represent a different part of the application. Let's look at the different Rails pieces these stories will require in more detail.

Defining the Resources

When you think about your application, it's best to first think in terms of resources. Rails 2 is a resource-centric development environment, so your development will usually begin by defining your resources. In precise terms, a resource is an Internet entity that has methods to represent and manage that entity. In more practical terms, a typical Rails resource is a database-backed model, controllers to manage that model, and views to represent one or more of those models to your users. After you've defined preliminary requirements, your next task is to determine the resources that your application will need. Look at the story list and concentrate on nouns. A few obvious candidates for Rails resources are *photos*, *slides*, *slideshows*, and *categories*. Certain relationships between them emerge:

- A *category* has many *photos*, and a *photo* can have one or more *categories*.
- A *category* can have other *categories*.
- A *slideshow* has many *slides*.
- A *slide* has one *photo*.

A simple diagram such as the one in Figure 2-1 helps to show the resources in your application and the relationships between them. For many-to-one relationships, we'll use an arrow to mean *belongs to*, so the arrow will point from the one to the many. Two-sided arrows are *many-to-many*, and a line without arrows shows a *one-to-one* relationship. We'll represent a tree with an arrow that points back to the originating class. Later, we'll use Active Record to define each relationship, but in this chapter, we'll just implement a very basic Active Record model with no embellishments. But to do anything with Active Record, you're going to need to define your database.

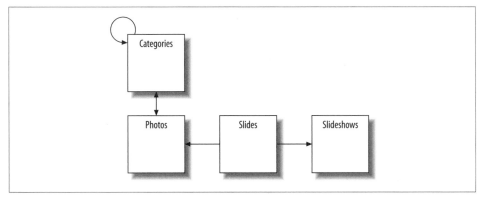

Figure 2-1. Scaffolding renders all four of these views

Preparing Your Project and Database

Before you can do anything, you'll need a Rails project. Create your project by typing **rails photos**, and then change into the new directory with cd photos. You'll see the following output, which we've abbreviated; your exact list may be different based on your version of Rails:

```
$ rails photos
      create
      create  app/controllers
      create  app/helpers
      create  app/models
...
      create  config/database.yml
      create  config/routes.rb
...

$ cd photos/
```

If your server is not started, restart it as usual with **script/server**. Point your browser to *http://localhost:3000/* to make sure things are working. You'll see the Rails welcome page if everything is working correctly.

Let's take a more detailed look at the files that Rails created with the new project. Notice that Rails created a database configuration file for you called *database.yml*. As of Rails 2, the default configuration file uses a lightweight database called *sqlite3*. You can use that database engine or another one, like MySQL. In this book, we'll use sqlite3. If you decide to use MySQL instead, you would need to install the database engine, and change *config/database.yml* to match your database configuration, which would look something like this:

```
development:
  adapter: mysql
  database: photos_development
  username: root
  password:
```

```
      host: localhost

test:
  adapter: mysql        test
  database: photos_development
  username: root
  password:
  host: localhost
```

If you choose to use MySQL or change your *database.yml* file in any way, keep in mind that in the data language called *YAML*, whitespace is significant. You'll want to indent with two spaces (not tabs) and make sure you don't have any trailing spaces on any of the lines. Check the MySQL documentation for instructions you can use to create a database called *photos_development* and another called *photos_test*. Otherwise, just keep the default configuration and you're off to the races.

Throughout the life of your project, you will use separate environments with separate databases to handle development, testing, and production deployment. Rails has its own strategy for dealing with test data that involves *deleting all test data between test runs*. You'll learn more about that later on. For now, just know that you should not configure your test database to point to any database with data that you want to keep!

 Do not configure your test database as your production or development database. All data in your test database is replaced each time you execute a new test.

Three Databases

Rails has three environments: *development*, *test*, and *production*. The Rails development environment reloads classes each time you call a new action, so you get a fresh copy of each class, including any recent development changes. The production environment loads classes once. With this approach, development performance is worse, but you get rapid turnaround time between making a change and seeing results in your browser while you develop your application. Rails reloads the test database before each test run, which works for testing but would be disastrous in production.

You also get separate development, production, and test databases. Sane developers don't want to use production databases to write code because they don't want to create, modify, or destroy production data. But why would Rails support a separate test database? In Chapter 7, you'll see that for each new test, Rails creates a fresh copy of test data, so each test case can modify database data without affecting other tests.

When Rails generates a new project, it creates a file called *database.yml*, with sections for development, test, and production. You'll need to keep a couple of things in mind as you configure a database. First, because Rails destroys the data in the test database, you need to make sure that you don't point this test configuration at your development

---

or production databases. Second, this file has passwords in plain text. Make sure you handle them appropriately.

Generating a Resource Scaffold

So far, you've already created your project and configured your database. The next step is to use scaffolding to generate a resource. We'll start with a simple photo. Initially, your photo will consist of an image in the filesystem and a record with an `id` and a filename in the database. Don't expect Rails to build you a complete production application. Code generators that try to do everything for you often lead to ugly complications when you're ready to enhance your app. We're looking for a head start that we can then customize. Let's scaffold up a resource for photos.

A List of Photos

The scaffold generator will build you a model, view, controller, and the tests to manage them. You can see the options for generating a scaffold by typing `script/generate scaffold`:

```
$ script/generate scaffold
Usage: script/generate scaffold ModelName [field:type, field:type]

Options:
        --skip-timestamps    Don't add timestamps to the migration file for this model
        --skip-migration     Don't generate a migration file for this model

Rails Info:
    -v, --version            Show the Rails version number and quit.
    -h, --help               Show this help message and quit.

General Options:
    -p, --pretend            Run but do not make any changes.
    -f, --force              Overwrite files that already exist.
    -s, --skip               Skip files that already exist.
    -q, --quiet              Suppress normal output.
    -t, --backtrace          Debugging: show backtrace on errors.
    -c, --svn                Modify files with subversion. (Note: svn must be in path)
    -g, --git                Modify files with git. (Note: git must be in path)

...
```

As you generate your scaffold, you can specify not only the name of the model, but also the fields that your model supports. Generate a scaffold for photos like this:

```
$ script/generate scaffold photo filename:string thumbnail:string description:string
...
      create    app/models/photo.rb
...
      create    db/migrate/20080427170510_create_photos.rb
```

In the script/generate command, you specified the name of the model and three columns that our application will need. Rails generated a bunch of files, including a controller and a a few views, but for a few moments, let's concentrate on the file called *app/models/photo.rb* and the file called *db/migrate/20080427170510_create_photos.rb*. The number in front of your create_photos.rb file will be different, but the rest should be the same. The first is an Active Record model. That file has this code:

```
class Photo < ActiveRecord::Base
end
```

Strangely, *photo.rb* does not have any information about the database table or any of its columns. You'll learn how Rails discovers these details in Chapter 3. You will need to create the table outside of the Active Record model. The best way is through a schema migration. As part of the resource scaffolding, Rails generated a default migration for you. The numbers before the migration are a timestamp. Rails will use these timestamps to help you apply incremental changes to your database schema as you need them, and back up one step should you make a serious mistake. To see how migrations work, first take a look at the migration that Rails created for you. Find the file that looks like *db/migrate/20080427170510_create_photos.rb*:

```
class CreatePhotos < ActiveRecord::Migration
  def self.up
    create_table :photos do |t|
      t.string :filename
      t.string :thumbnail
      t.string :description

      t.timestamps
    end
  end

  def self.down
    drop_table :photos
  end
end
```

The migration has an up and a down method. Each method makes a change to the existing database schema. up makes changes forward in time, and down makes changes backward in time. Think of the up method as a do, and the down method as an undo. In this case, the up method creates a table, and the down method drops that table. You can indicate options after each column specification that allow you to specify table attributes such as non-nullable columns (:null => false), default values (:default => ""), and the like. You can see how migrations move forward by running the command rake db:migrate:

```
$ rake db:migrate
(in /Users/lance/Projects/book/repo/current/src/chapter2/photos)
== 20080427170510 CreatePhotos: migrating =====================================
-- create_table(:photos)
   -> 0.0047s
== 20080427170510 CreatePhotos: migrated (0.0049s) ============================
```

rake is the Ruby utility that helps you manage all things that are related to the application itself. Both Java (ant) and C (make) have similar utilities. Throughout this book, you'll use *rake* tasks to run tests, load test data, change your database schema, and many other things. In this case, the db:migrate task runs all migrations that have not yet been run. Rails makes a note of each migration that has been run in the schema_migrations table:

```
$ sqlite3 db/development.sqlite3
SQLite version 3.4.0
Enter ".help" for instructions
sqlite> select * from schema_migrations;
20080427170510
```

Type .quit to exit sqlite3.

As you can see, Rails creates one line in the schema_migrations table for each migrated table. The next time you run rake db:migrate, Rails will run the up methods on all migrations that are not listed in the table, with those with the earliest timestamps running first. You can also migrate down. You can specify a specific version number by typing rake db:migrate VERSION=<a-timestamp> where <a-timestamp> is the timestamp of one of your migrations. You can also run the up or down method on a specific migration. Try it now (remember, your timestamp will be different):

```
$ rake db:migrate:down VERSION=20080427170510
(in /Users/lance/Projects/book/repo/current/src/chapter2/photos)
== 20080427170510 CreatePhotos: reverting =====================================
-- drop_table(:photos)
   -> 0.0031s
== 20080427170510 CreatePhotos: reverted (0.0032s) ============================

$ rake db:migrate:up VERSION=20080427170510
(in /Users/lance/Projects/book/repo/current/src/chapter2/photos)
== 20080427170510 CreatePhotos: migrating =====================================
-- create_table(:photos)
   -> 0.0044s
== 20080427170510 CreatePhotos: migrated (0.0046s) ============================
```

You now have a working model. It would be nice to have some test data. One of the easiest ways to create test data is to use the fixtures that Rails uses for unit tests. We'll discuss the pros and cons of testing in Chapter 7, but for now, just edit the file *test/ fixtures/photos.yml* to look like this:

```
photo_1:
  id: 1
  filename: train.jpg
  thumbnail: train_t.jpg
  description: My ride to work

photo_2:
  id: 2
  filename: lighthouse.jpg
  thumbnail: lighthouse_t.jpg
  description: I take dates here all the time
```

```
photo_3:
  id: 3
  filename: gargoyle.jpg
  thumbnail: gargoyle_t.jpg
  description: My paper weight

photo_4:
  id: 4
  filename: cat.jpg
  thumbnail: cat_t.jpg
  description: My pet

photo_5:
  id: 5
  filename: cappucino.jpg
  thumbnail: cappucino_t.jpg
  description: Life juice

photo_6:
  id: 6
  filename: building.jpg
  thumbnail: building_t.jpg
  description: My office

photo_7:
  id: 7
  filename: bridge.jpg
  thumbnail: bridge_t.jpg
  description: A place I'd like to visit

photo_8:
  id: 8
  filename: bear.jpg
  thumbnail: bear_t.jpg
  description: Day at the zoo

photo_9:
  id: 9
  filename: baskets.jpg
  thumbnail: baskets_t.jpg
  description: Where I store my fruit
```

You can specify your test data in the YAML language. Remember, YAML is sensitive to whitespace, so be careful. You can load the data with a simple **rake** command called **db:fixtures:load**. Do that now:

```
$ rake db:fixtures:load
(in /Users/lance/Projects/book/repo/current/src/chapter2/photos)
```

As you follow along, at some point you might find it useful to start over, dropping all database tables, running all migrations, and loading your test data from scratch. That could happen if you have a coding error in a migration that partially completes. You may find that you're unable to migrate down because your migrations try to drop a table that does not exist. You can't proceed, either, because one of your tables doesn't exist as it should—you'd have to hack your database by hand. There's a better way. You can build a rake task to wipe out the database, run all of your migrations from scratch, and then load your test data. Rake tasks go in *lib/tasks*. Create a file called *lib/tasks/photos.rake* that looks like this:

```
namespace :photos do
  desc "Reset the photos application environment"
  task :reset => :environment do
    Rake::Task["db:migrate:reset"].invoke
    Rake::Task["db:fixtures:load"].invoke
  end
end
```

You've actually built a custom rake task called reset in the namespace photos. A namespace is simply a way to organize like rake tasks. You can invoke the task by typing rake photos:reset.

```
$ rake photos:reset
(in /Users/lance/Projects/book/repo/current/src/chapter2/photos)
== 20080427170510 CreatePhotos: migrating ======================================
-- create_table(:photos)
   -> 0.0036s
== 20080427170510 CreatePhotos: migrated (0.0038s) =============================
```

Depending on your platform, you may get a warning that the database already exists. If you do, just ignore it. The task executes two other rake tasks: db:migrate:reset (dropping all database tables and deleting rows in schema_migrations) and db:fixtures:load. The tasks depend on another rake task called environment, which loads the appropriate environment. In our case, the environment will usually be the development environment.

That's all you need for a working photos scaffold. Rails has already done the rest. Now, load the URL *http://localhost:3000/photos* to see the scaffolding in action. You'll see a list of photos with links to create new photos, and to edit and show existing ones. With the scaffolding generator, you get all of the pages shown in Figure 2-1. The scaffolding generates surprisingly complete controller and view codes. To be sure, the scaffolding does not generate production-ready code, but it's a starting point. The next section will scaffold slides and dive a little into REST and routes. Let's move on.

 If you get the following error when trying to access the application:

```
Mysql::Error in Photo#list
Access denied for user: 'root@localhost' (Using password: NO)
```

it means that you forgot to restart the server after you configured the database.

RESTful Routes

Now that you have a working scaffold for photos, we can move on to slides. In this section, we'll create another default scaffold, but we'll concentrate on the controllers, and the routes that Rails will use to access each resource. As you recall, a route tells Rails how to interpret an incoming URL. Given a route and a URL, Rails can determine:

- The parameters that Rails will pass to the controller via the **params** hash
- The controller Rails will access (stored in **params[:controller]**)
- The action that Rails will invoke (stored in **params[:action]**)

Let's see REST and routes in action. First, generate the scaffolding for a slide:

```
$ script/generate scaffold slide position:integer photo_id:integer slideshow_id:integer
...
      create  app/views/slides
      create  app/views/slides/index.html.erb
      create  app/views/slides/show.html.erb
      create  app/views/slides/new.html.erb
      create  app/views/slides/edit.html.erb
      create  app/views/layouts/slides.html.erb
...
      create  app/controllers/slides_controller.rb
      create  test/functional/slides_controller_test.rb
...
       route  map.resources :slides
...
```

As you learned last time, Rails creates a bunch of files for you. This time, we'll focus on the controllers, views, and the route. As before, a little test data will make it easier to test the application. This time, we're going to take advantage of templating features. Ruby's ERb interprets the fixture files just like it does views. Edit *test/fixtures/ slides.yml* to look like this:

```
<% 1.upto(9) do |i| %>
slide_<%= i %>:
  id: <%= i %>
  position: <%= i %>
  photo_id: <%= i %>
  slideshow_id: 1
<% end %>
```

Everywhere you see code bracketed by <% and %>, ERb will execute that Ruby code and show nothing in its place. Everywhere you see code bracketed by <%= and %>, ERb will execute the code and replace the code with the return value of the operation. This fixture is equivalent to the following static stencil:

```
slide_1:
  id: 1
  position: 1
  photo_id: 1
  slideshow_id: 1
```

```
slide_2:
  id: 2
  position: 2
  photo_id: 2
  slideshow_id: 1
```

```
... and so on ...
```

Run **rake photos:reset** to load your data. You have a working resource for slides, complete with a full set of sample data that has an identical set of screens to the photos scaffold. Let's look under the covers at the routes. We'll use this scaffold in our REST conversation later, but now we need to lay some groundwork with named routes.

Named Routes

Now, let's shift our attention to named routes. Let's generate another scaffold, this time for slideshows. Type **... script/generate scaffold slideshow name:string**.

```
   exists  app/models/
   exists  app/controllers/
   exists  app/helpers/
...
   route  map.resources :slideshows
...
```

Run `rake db:migrate` to create your database tables as always. Notice the `route` command. This command creates some specific URL patterns that your application will use. Let's back up a minute to explain.

Every Rails command maps onto one of the routes specified in *config/routes.rb*. In Chapter 1, though we didn't explain it, Rails generated a route that looked like `map.connect ':controller/:action/:id'`. Each time Rails encountered a URL of the form */controller/action/id*, Rails parsed the URL into a hash called `params` having keys `:controller`, `:action`, and `:id` with the corresponding values from the URL.

But now, turn your attention to the `route map.resources :slideshows` statement in *config/routes.rb*. When you generated the scaffold, Rails added a line to *routes.rb*. Open that file now. You'll find the following statements near the top of the file:

```
map.resources :slideshows
```

```
map.resources :slides
```

```
map.resources :photos
```

The statement `map.resources :slideshows` actually builds eight complex routes that you can refer to by name. You can see all of the routes, in the order that Rails will try to match, by typing `rake routes`. Among others, you'll see the routes that Rails added for slideshows. These are the main routes without the format routes that are close cousins of the named routes below:

```
slideshows
  GET /slideshows
   {:action=>"index", :controller=>"slideshows"}

  POST /slideshows
   {:action=>"create", :controller=>"slideshows"}

new_slideshow
  GET /slideshows/new
   {:action=>"new", :controller=>"slideshows"}

edit_slideshow
  GET /slideshows/:id/edit
   {:action=>"edit", :controller=>"slideshows"}

slideshow
  GET /slideshows/:id
   {:action=>"show", :controller=>"slideshows"}

  PUT /slideshows/:id
   {:action=>"update", :controller=>"slideshows"}

  DELETE /slideshows/:id
   {:action=>"destroy", :controller=>"slideshows"}
```

To fully understand what's going on here, we'll need to review a little bit about HTTP. Most web developers know that the HTTP protocol supports at least two verbs: GET and POST. Normally, when your browser loads a URL, it uses an HTTP GET. When it submits a form, it uses an HTTP POST. You might not know that HTTP also supports at least two other verbs: PUT and DELETE, even though most browsers don't support those last two.

Now you can make a little more sense out of the list. You see four named routes in this list: slideshows, new_slideshow, edit_slideshow, and slideshow. (The actual output of rake routes has eight named routes, with a formatted version of all of the above named routes. Those routes help Rails process file formats such as XML, but disregard the formatted routes for now.) Notice that each name is followed by an HTTP request composed of a verb, a URL, and the mapping that Rails will use for the request. This rule shows that *a route depends on the HTTP verb*. For example, an HTTP request to GET /slideshows/4 will invoke the show method on the slideshows controller, but PUT /slideshows/4 will invoke the update action instead.

REST

I promised you a brief introduction to REST in this chapter, and it's a good time to return to that conversation. Think of REST as a way of looking at HTTP as a collection of resources. Think of the HTTP verbs as the Internet version of the database CRUD methods:

- *Create:* POST
- *Read:* GET
- *Update:* PUT
- *Delete:* DELETE

You can see that the Rails routes map to this concept perfectly. Armed with the pre-defined named routes, you can do any REST operation. In fact, you can probably guess the controller actions that the scaffolding generator created for you. To confirm your suspicions, crack open *app/controllers/slides_controller.rb*. We won't list all of the code right now, or try to explain it. For now, just look at the methods that the controller supports and the comments that accompany each method:

```ruby
class SlidesController < ApplicationController
  # GET /slides
  # GET /slides.xml
  def index
    ...
  end

  # GET /slides/1
  # GET /slides/1.xml
  def show
    ...
  end

  # GET /slides/new
  # GET /slides/new.xml
  def new
    ...
  end

  # GET /slides/1/edit
  def edit
    ...
  end

  # POST /slides
  # POST /slides.xml
  def create
    ...
  end

  # PUT /slides/1
  # PUT /slides/1.xml
  def update
    ...
  end

  # DELETE /slides/1
  # DELETE /slides/1.xml
  def destroy
    ...
```

```
    end
  end
```

These methods perfectly correspond to the named routes created in `routes.rb` and listed in `rake routes`. The comments simply serve to remind you about the named routes. You know that a GET to *http://your_application/slides/new* will fire the `new` action (remember, a method on a controller implements an action), and a POST to `/slides` will fire the `create` action.

In fact, simple Table 2-1 shows you the mapping between the HTTP method, the Rails action, and the database. When you learn to think of every Internet application as a collection of resources, your applications often get much simpler.

Table 2-1. REST verbs with their associated Rails methods and database commands

	Create	Read	Update	Delete
HTTP	POST	GET	PUT	DELETE
Rails	CREATE	SHOW	UPDATE	DESTROY
Database	INSERT	SELECT	UPDATE	DELETE

Let us cover one more idea before moving on. In Rails, you should think of the `edit` and `update` actions as a pair. `edit` renders a form that a user can use to update a slide. Submitting the form calls the `update` action, which validates the transaction and updates the item in the database. The `new` and `create` methods work together the same way. We'll dive into the individual code for each controller method in much more detail throughout the rest of the book. For now, you can take the application for a test drive in the console. Think of the console as a command line for your application. First, edit *app/controllers/slides_controller.rb* and add the `skip_before_filter` line:

```
class SlidesController < ApplicationController
  skip_before_filter :verify_authenticity_token
  ...
```

This disables the request verification token, a new feature in rails that ensures the request is made from your application. You should remove this line after you run the following commands in your console. Put your newly acquired REST knowledge to work:

```
$ script/console
Loading development environment (Rails 2.1.0)
>> app.get "/slides"
=> 200
>> app.request.path_parameters
=> {"action"=>"index", "controller"=>"slides"}
>> app.get "/slides/1"
=> 200
>> app.request.path_parameters
=> {"action"=>"show", "id"=>"1", "controller"=>"slides"}
>> app.post "/slides", :slide => {:position => 10, :photo_id => 1, :slideshow_id => 1}
=> 302
```

```
>> app.request.path_parameters
=> {"action"=>"create", "controller"=>"slides"}
>> app.put "/slides/1", :slide => {:position => 1, :photo_id => 1, :slideshow_id => 2}
=> 302
>> app.request.path_parameters
=> {"action"=>"update", "id"=>"1", "controller"=>"slides"}
>> app.delete "/slides/10"
=> 302
>> app.request.path_parameters
=> {"action"=>"destroy", "id"=>"10", "controller"=>"slides"}
```

Using these techniques, you can exercise your application just as if you were calling it over the Internet. You can send HTTP commands to your application through commands such as `app.get`. Remember, the return code for a successful HTTP command is `200`, and the return code for an HTTP redirect command is a `302`. The `path_parameters` command shows you the actual parameters that Rails would pass to the controller in the `params` hash. If you wanted to, you could also see the `app.response.body` after any request, and it would contain the web page that Rails would create. Remove the `skip_before_filter` after you're done testing the console.

The Controller Code

Let's review what you know. Whenever you type a Rails URL, your web server, Mongrel, takes the request and forwards it to Rails. The Rails router finds a route that matches the request, creates a `params` hash, and then invokes your controller. Let's take a brief look at the default controller code. We haven't learned anything about Active Record yet, but that's OK. We'll just gloss over that code at a high level before hitting it in detail in Chapters 3 and 4. We'll look at a few actions at a time. Let's start with the simplest, the `show` action in `app/controllers/slideshows_controller.rb`:

```
# GET /slideshows/1
# GET /slideshows/1.xml
def show
  @slideshow = Slideshow.find(params[:id])

  respond_to do |format|
    format.html # show.html.erb
    format.xml  { render :xml => @slideshow }
  end
end
```

The comments tell you exactly how the named routes behave. A `GET` request to `slideshows/1` or `/slideshows/1.xml` will invoke this controller action. Invoking `/slideshows/1.xml` would result in the following `params` hash:

```
params
{
  :controller => 'slideshows',
  :action => 'show',
  :id => '1',
```

```
    :format => 'xml'
  }
```

When you omit the .xml or .html, the default format is html.
@slideshow = Slideshow.find(params[:id]) is straightforward, though you have not
seen Active Record yet. Rails will find a Slideshow with the id in the params hash. The
next lines of code are a little more complicated because you have a nested code block:

```
respond_to do |format|
  format.html # show.html.erb
  format.xml  { render :xml => @slideshow }
end
```

This code is a way to conditionally execute code based on the format of a request.
respond_to is a Rails method that will conditionally execute the code block beside the
appropriate format statement. When params[:format] is xml, Rails executes render :xml
=> @slideshow, and when params[:format] is html, Rails will do nothing. Remember,
when an action doesn't explicitly call render, Rails simply renders the default view. So,
a simplified view that services only HTML requests would look like this:

```
def show
  @slideshow = Slideshow.find(params[:id])
  # show.html.erb
end
```

The controller action for index works exactly the same way, but index finds all slideshows instead of just one. The code for destroy is slightly different:

```
def destroy
  @slideshow = Slideshow.find(params[:id])
  @slideshow.destroy

  respond_to do |format|
    format.html { redirect_to(slideshows_url) }
    format.xml  { head :ok }
  end
end
```

Rather than rendering an action, destroy does a redirect to slideshows_url, which is a
named route for the index action.

Two of the remaining actions are dead simple. They render forms for creating and
updating slideshows. They are the new and edit actions:

```
# GET /slideshows/new
# GET /slideshows/new.xml
def new
  @slideshow = Slideshow.new

  respond_to do |format|
    format.html # new.html.erb
    format.xml  { render :xml => @slideshow }
  end
end
```

```
# GET /slideshows/1/edit
def edit
  @slideshow = Slideshow.find(params[:id])
end
```

edit just finds the existing slideshow and renders the form. new creates a blank object and renders the form or XML for the empty item. In practice, you would rarely call new with an xml format. Submitting the edit form for a Slideshow with an id of 1 will make the HTTP request PUT slideshows/1, invoking the update action and passing the new attributes for the Slideshow in params:

```
# PUT /slideshows/1
# PUT /slideshows/1.xml
def update
  @slideshow = Slideshow.find(params[:id])

  respond_to do |format|
    if @slideshow.update_attributes(params[:slideshow])
      flash[:notice] = 'Slideshow was successfully updated.'
      format.html { redirect_to(@slideshow) }
      format.xml  { head :ok }
    else
      format.html { render :action => "edit" }
      format.xml  {
        render :xml => @slideshow.errors,
          :status => :unprocessable_entity
      }
    end
  end
end
```

This code is a little more complicated than the rest because it must deal with error conditions across two formats. Still, it's remarkably simple. Keep in mind that params[:slideshow] contains another hash with all of the attributes from the edit form. The update method finds a slideshow with @slideshow = Slideshow.find(params[:id]). Then, in a respond_to code block, the method tries to update the attributes in @slideshow with the parameters in the params[:slideshow] hash. If successful, Rails sends a message to the user in a temporary holding area called the flash, and redirects for HTML or renders a brief status message in XML. If the update is not successful, the code renders a view that's appropriate to the format. The create method works almost exactly the same way.

We've come a long way in a short time. We'll be modifying these actions and diving into more details behind the views and controllers, so it's OK if you don't perfectly understand everything yet. For now, just understand that you have working models, views, and controllers that will serve as the foundation for the application in the rest of the book.

Wrapping Up the Scaffolding

Whew. That section had a lot of detail. Now we have only to scaffold the last resource for categories and create the test data for slideshows and categories. Generate the scaffold for categories now with the following command in your terminal:

```
$ script/generate scaffold category parent_id:integer name:string
...
      create  app/views/categories
      create  app/views/categories/index.html.erb
      create  app/views/categories/show.html.erb
      create  app/views/categories/new.html.erb
      create  app/views/categories/edit.html.erb
      create  app/views/layouts/categories.html.erb
   identical  public/stylesheets/scaffold.css
      create  app/controllers/categories_controller.rb
      create  test/functional/categories_controller_test.rb
      create  app/helpers/categories_helper.rb
       route  map.resources :categories
  dependency  model
...
      create  app/models/category.rb
      create  test/unit/category_test.rb
      create  test/fixtures/categories.yml
      create  db/migrate/20080509013624_create_categories.rb
```

Rails creates the usual suspects. We've shortened the listing, but you get the idea. Rails creates your controller, views, a named route, and test code for Category. As always, create the test fixtures with the data below. text/fixtures/slideshows.yml should like like the following:

```
slideshow_1:
  id: 1
  name: Interesting Pictures
```

and text/fixtures/categories.yml should look like the following:

```
category_1:
  id: 1
  name: All
category_2:
  id: 2
  parent_id: 1
  name: People
category_3:
  id: 3
  parent_id: 1
  name: Animals
category_4:
  id: 4
  parent_id: 1
  name: Places
category_5:
  id: 5
  parent_id: 1
```

```
      name: Things
  category_6:
    id: 6
    parent_id: 2
    name: Friends
  category_7:
    id: 7
    parent_id: 2
    name: Family
```

Finally, you can run the migration and load the test data with `rake photos:reset`. That's it. The scaffolding is all done. When you filter out the explanation text, you can see that in a very short time you've built some pretty sophisticated views that can service both XML and HTML requests.

What's Next?

You've created a full-featured Rails application, but the models are pretty primitive so far. A slideshow does not know that it is composed of slides, and a photo does not have any relationship with categories. In the next few chapters, you're going to learn to put Active Record through its paces. You'll learn the features we need to implement PhotoShare, and a few more Active Record features. Let's fire up your chosen database engine and get to work.

## CHAPTER 3

Active Record Basics

In Chapter 1, you learned that Rails is a framework for building database-backed web applications. Active Record handles the database-backed part. Active Record uses convention instead of configuration whenever possible, and uses the capabilities of Ruby to dynamically add attributes and methods to your models based on the contents of the database. But this amazing framework is dead simple. In this chapter, you'll build a few database classes with a mere handful of lines of configuration code. You'll also see firsthand how Ruby's metaprogramming will add methods and attributes to your classes based on the contents and structure of the database. Finally, you'll use Active Record's built-in language to validate your code quickly with just a few trivial lines of code. First, a little background is in order.

Active Record Basics

Martin Fowler cataloged the Active Record design pattern in a book called *Patterns of Enterprise Application Architecture* (Addison-Wesley).* The Rails framework is an implementation of that idea. With any Active Record implementation, classes represent database tables, and instances (called record objects) represent database rows. Each Active Record object has CRUD (Create, Read, Update, and Delete) methods for database access. This strategy allows simple designs and straightforward mappings between database tables and application objects.

The Rails implementation of Active Record is like Martin Fowler's pattern on steroids. The Rails version adds some capabilities that extend Active Record. Rails adds attributes automatically, based on the columns in the database. That feature means you will specify your attributes exactly once, when you define your schema in your schema migration. Rails also adds relationship management and validation through a custom language so you can add rich behavior to their model objects to manage relationships and validations without an excessive amount of code, configuration, or code

---

* Design patterns in *Patterns of Enterprise Architecture* appear in an online catalog. The Active Record pattern is defined at *http://www.martinfowler.com/eaaCatalog/activeRecord.html*.

generation. Finally, the Rails implementation uses naming conventions that let Active Record discover table names and specific fields, so much of what you do will require very little extra code and configuration. Don't worry. You can still drop down to SQL if you ever need to.

Wrapping, Not Mapping

With some other database frameworks, you independently build a database table and an object. You then build a map between the two with code or configuration, often written in XML. We call this strategy *object relational mapping* (ORM), and such frameworks are *mapping* frameworks. Java developers usually favor ORM because it can support various kinds of database schemas, including legacy schemas with many different strategies for building a schema. The drawback to ORM is that your code has more repetition because you often need to specify column information in your database schema and in your code.

But Active Record is a *wrapping* framework, not a *mapping* framework. With Rails, you'll start by building a relational database table with a schema migration and wrapping each table with an Active Record class. Each class represents a table, and each instance represents a row of the database. The framework then automatically discovers columns from the database table and dynamically adds them to the Active Record class. Using Active Record, you can build a simple mapping to a typical table in two lines of code.

A Brief Example

When you built your scaffold in Chapter 2, you generated an Active Record model. Here's a slightly modified version of that class:

```
class Photo < ActiveRecord::Base
  belongs_to :category
end
```

In this Active Record chapter, we're going to talk about everything that happens automatically when you define the class. In the next chapter, we'll dive into relationships between the classes, such as the `belongs_to` class that you've just seen. This Active Record class is surprisingly complete. There are only a few lines of code, no configuration at all, and no duplication between the model and the schema. Let's break it down:

```
class Photo < ActiveRecord::Base
```

We define a class called `Photo` that's a subclass of the `Base` class in the `ActiveRecord` module. From naming conventions and the name `Photo`, Active Record infers that this class wraps a database table called `photos`. The name provides enough information to let the `Base` class query the database engine for all of the columns of the `photos` table. `Base` then adds metadata from each column—such as column names, types, and lengths—to `Photo`. Based on that metadata, `Base` then adds an attribute to `Photo` for each column in the database. Let's move on to the next slice of code:

```
belongs_to :category
```

This code fragment is an example of a *domain-specific language* (DSL), a language built for a narrow purpose. You'll use this DSL to specify relationships between your models. Chapter 4 will walk you through these relationships in much more detail. A similar language will help you handle validations. `belongs_to` is actually a method of `Base`, and `:category` is a Ruby symbol. The `belongs_to` command changes the `Photo` class, adding all of the methods and attributes you'll need to handle a many-to-one relationship between `Photo` and `Category`. Through naming conventions, `Base` discovers the column responsible for managing the relationship. For example, you'll learn later that each `Photo` object has an attribute called `category`. Updating `photo.category` will automatically change the foreign key, called `category_id`, in the database. So, while this relationship seems trivial to implement, it adds great power to Photo Share. By creating the above code, all of the following examples are possible on `photo`, an instance of `Photo`:

- `photo.category = Category.new`. This example assigns an Active Record object of type Category to the photo, based on the `belongs_to :category` relationship.

- `photo.filename`. If the database table `photos` has a column called `filename`, `photo` objects will all have the filename attribute.

- `photo.save`, `photo.destroy`, `photo.update_attribute('filename', 'new Value.gif')`. You can save, delete, and update all photos.

- `photo = Photo.find_by_filename('cat.jpg')`. You can find a new photo by id, or by any of the existing attributes. You will also learn how to do more complex finds later.

- `photo.to_xml`. You can translate any model to XML and a few other formats.

With just a few short lines of code, Active Record can infer your intent and make each line of code work harder for you. In the chapters to come, you'll learn to use the simple models that you already built in Chapter 2. Let's get started.

Generating Models

When you generated a scaffold, Rails created a model for you. You can use the `script/generate` command to create models without building the whole resource. As always, you can let the `script/generate` command tell you the basics:

```
$ script/generate model
Usage: script/generate model ModelName [field:type, field:type]

Options:
        --skip-timestamps    Don't add timestamps to the migration file for this model
        --skip-migration     Don't generate a migration file for this model
        --skip-fixture       Don't generation a fixture file for this model
```

```
Rails Info:
    -v, --version            Show the Rails version number and quit.
    -h, --help               Show this help message and quit.

General Options:
    -p, --pretend            Run but do not make any changes.
    -f, --force              Overwrite files that already exist.
    -s, --skip               Skip files that already exist.
    -q, --quiet              Suppress normal output.
    -t, --backtrace          Debugging: show backtrace on errors.
    -c, --svn                Modify files with subversion. (Note: svn must be in path)
    -g, --git                Modify files with git. (Note: git must be in path)

Description:
    Stubs out a new model. Pass the model name, either CamelCased or
    under_scored, and an optional list of attribute pairs as arguments.

    Attribute pairs are column_name:sql_type arguments specifying the
    model's attributes. Timestamps are added by default, so you don't have to
    specify them by hand as 'created_at:datetime updated_at:datetime'.

    You don't have to think up every attribute up front, but it helps to
    sketch out a few so you can start working with the model immediately.

    This generates a model class in app/models, a unit test in test/unit,
    a test fixture in test/fixtures/singular_name.yml, and a migration in
    db/migrate.

Examples:
    `./script/generate model account`

        creates an Account model, test, fixture, and migration:
            Model:      app/models/account.rb
            Test:       test/unit/account_test.rb
            Fixtures:   test/fixtures/accounts.yml
            Migration:  db/migrate/XXX_add_accounts.rb

    `./script/generate model post title:string body:text published:boolean`

        creates a Post model with a string title, text body, and published flag.
```

You can see the syntax for generating models and scaffolds. Just for kicks, generate a model for real:

```
$ script/generate model user login:string password:string
        exists  app/models/
        exists  test/unit/
        exists  test/fixtures/
        create  app/models/user.rb
        create  test/unit/user_test.rb
        create  test/fixtures/users.yml
        exists  db/migrate
        create  db/migrate/20080510162859_create_users.rb
```

The **generate** command created a schema migration, a model, a unit test, and fixtures. You've already used most of those files. Take a second look at the migration and model. Here are the files *app/models/user.rb* and *db/migrate/20080510162859_create_users.rb* (remember, your timestamp before **_create_users** will be different):

```
class User < ActiveRecord::Base
end

db/migrate/20080510162859_create_users.rb
class CreateUsers < ActiveRecord::Migration
  def self.up
    create_table :users do |t|
      t.string :login
      t.string :password

      t.timestamps
    end
  end

  def self.down
    drop_table :users
  end
end
```

Rails completely separates the database schema from the model class. You'll specify the column data in exactly one place: your database schema migration. Rails uses that migration to create an up-to-date schema. But we don't really need a User model. Delete it with **script/destroy**:

```
$ script/destroy model user
    notempty  db/migrate
    notempty  db
         rm   db/migrate/20080510162859_create_users.rb
         rm   test/fixtures/users.yml
         rm   test/unit/user_test.rb
         rm   app/models/user.rb
    notempty  test/fixtures
    notempty  test
    notempty  test/unit
    notempty  test
    notempty  app/models
    notempty  app
```

The generation of the model, migration, and unit test with fixtures is a tremendous time-saver. You can let Rails handle the drudgery of creating the migration and the templates for your model and test. You can concentrate on coding only the unique slices of your application.

It's time to flip back over to Photo Share again. Recall that we already have working database-backed models for photos, slides, slideshows, and categories, but it's been some time since we worked with them. You could use a quick refresher for what we've done so far. If you ever need a bird's eye view of the whole application, you can see the whole database schema at a glance in the *db/schema.rb* file. Make sure your migrations are up-to-date by running `rake photos:reset`. Then, open *db/schema.rb*:[*]

```
$ rake photos:reset
(in /Users/lancelotcarlson/Projects/book/repo/current/src/chapter3/photos)
== 20080427170510 CreatePhotos: migrating ====================================
-- create_table(:photos)
   -> 0.0032s
== 20080427170510 CreatePhotos: migrated (0.0034s) ===========================

== 20080427174033 CreateSlides: migrating ====================================
-- create_table(:slides)
   -> 0.0033s
== 20080427174033 CreateSlides: migrated (0.0035s) ===========================

== 20080428012614 CreateSlideshows: migrating ================================
-- create_table(:slideshows)
   -> 0.0032s
== 20080428012614 CreateSlideshows: migrated (0.0069s) =======================

== 20080509013624 CreateCategories: migrating ================================
-- create_table(:categories)
   -> 0.0033s
== 20080509013624 CreateCategories: migrated (0.0035s) =======================
```

With that listing, you can see the complete list of tables and the columns that each table supports. Some Active Record features take a little getting used to. Looking at a model without all of the attributes at your fingertips is strange. Having a complete list of tables and attributes in *db/schema.rb* helps alleviate that pain by giving you a single source with the names and types of all attributes. We're finally ready to put the models through their paces.

Basic Active Record Classes

As you create new database tables, you'll want to use a couple of common naming conventions. The table name `photos` and the definition of the id column are both significant. (With our migration, Rails created the id column automatically.) Rails uses several naming conventions:

Class and table names

If the name of your database tables is the English plural of the name of your model class, Rails can usually infer the name of the database table from the name of the Active Record class. (Active Record will have trouble with some irregulars such as moose, but supports many popular irregulars such as people.)

---

[*] If you're coding along with us by hand, make sure the code is exactly as we left it at the end of Chapter 2. If you're not sure, download the program listing from *http://www.oreilly.com/catalog/9780596522001*. The file for Chapter 2 will have the `photos` application state after the completion of Chapter 2. Download the code, migrate, and run `rake photos:reset` to run your migrations from scratch and load your test data.

Identifiers

Similarly, Active Record automatically finds a column called `id` and uses it as a unique identifier. The `id` column should be an integer type and be populated by the database. In this case, the migration creates a SQLite auto-increment sequence. Staying with these conventions saves you some configuration, and it also makes your code much easier to understand.

Foreign keys

Foreign keys should be named `<class>_id`. For example, our `slides` table will have a foreign key named `photo_id` to refer to a row in the `photos` table.

Capitalization

When you're defining a class, use standard Ruby conventions. Capitalize the first letter of each word and omit spaces between words (commonly called *camel casing*). But Rails methods, database table names, columns, attributes, and symbols use underscores to separate words. These conventions are mostly cosmetic, but Rails often uses symbols to refer to a class name, so make sure you follow these conventions. For example, to represent a class called `ChunkyBacon`, you'd use the symbol `:chunky_bacon`.

Wrapping the Table

Now we're ready to look at the Active Record model class that Rails generated earlier. In the *app/models* directory (which contains all of your project's model classes), Rails created the *app/models/photo.rb* file. Open it:

```
class Photo < ActiveRecord::Base
end
```

The `ActiveRecord::Base` class has all of the information that it needs to wrap the photos table. It's time to take the new classes for a test drive.

The Rails Console

We introduced the Rails console in Chapter 2. If you want to rapidly improve as a Rails programmer, spend as much time as you can within it, especially as you work with your Active Record models. From a database perspective, the Rails console lets you interactively work with your database-backed models using the same code that you'll use later in your controllers. Whether you're testing out methods or doing data transformation, this simple tool will be invaluable. When you start a console, Rails does the following:

- Connects you to the database
- Loads the Active Record classes in *app/model*
- Lets you interactively work with your model, including database operations

You can have Rails reload all of your models at any time by using the **reload!** command. Let's start a console now to manipulate the Photo model we created:

```
$ script/console
```

We'll use the console to create some new Photo objects, and save them to the database:[*]

```
>> photo = Photo.new
=> #<Photo id: nil, filename: nil, thumbnail: nil, description: nil,
created_at: nil, updated_at: nil>
>> photo.filename = 'cat.jpg'
=> "cat.jpg"
>> photo.save
=> true
>> photo.inspect
=> "#<Photo id: 10, filename: \"cat.jpg\", thumbnail: nil, description: nil,
created_at: \"2008-05-10 12:40:23\", updated_at: \"2008-05-10 12:40:23\">"
```

You can also create rows in other ways. **create** takes a hash map and automatically does a save. The **new** method can take a code block, which takes an argument of the new object:

```
>> Photo.create(:filename => 'dog.jpg')
=> #<Photo id: 11, filename: "dog.jpg", thumbnail: nil, description: nil,
created_at: "2008-05-10 12:29:29", updated_at: "2008-05-10 12:29:29">
>> Photo.new do |photo|
?>    photo.filename = 'armadillo.jpg'
>>    photo.save
>> end
=> #<Photo id: 12, filename: "armadillo.jpg", thumbnail: nil, description: nil,
created_at: "2008-05-10 12:43:49", updated_at: "2008-05-10 12:43:49">
```

Notice that the **create** method returns the new object, and you can see all of the attributes from the database. Remember, your model object did not have any of these attributes. Once again, it's time to look under the hood.

Attributes

We use the term metaprogramming often in this book, and now you've seen it in action. In this case, metaprogramming means that Active Record adds attributes and methods to your code based on the structure of the database without you writing any code. In the end, you'll code far less, but you'll have to work a little harder to understand the magic that goes on under the covers. Once you understand how Active Record works, you will know exactly what attributes and methods your model supports. And that's the secret to using Active Record.

---

[*] After each statement you type, the console will print the value of object.inspect, a convenient string-like representation of an object, for the last object returned.

Columns

Let's review what happens when Ruby loads the `Photo` class. The `Photo` class inherits from the `ActiveRecord::Base` class. When that class loads from the class name `Photo`, Active Record infers that the class wraps a database table named `photos`. `Base` then queries SQLite to retrieve information about the `photos` table, including the definition of each of the columns in that table. Next, `Base` saves the definition of each column into the `@@columns` class variable. (A class variable has a single value that all instances of the class share.) `@@columns` is an array of `Column` objects, with each column having these attributes:

name
> The name of the database column.

type
> The Ruby type of the attribute this column will generate.

number
> A Boolean value that's `true` if the column's data is numeric. You'll access it through the accessor method `number?`.

limit
> The maximum size of the data element. For example, for a database column of type `varchar(45)`, the limit would be 45.

null
> A Boolean value that's `true` only if the column can be set to `null`. You'll access it through the accessor method `null?`.

text
> A Boolean value that's `true` only if the column can be interpreted as text. You'll access it through the accessor `text?`.

default
> The default value you specified in the table definition.

primary
> A Boolean value that's `true` if the column is the Rails unique identifier. You'll access it through the accessor method `primary?`.

Sometimes your applications can use this column metadata to build dynamic user interfaces. Earlier versions of the scaffolding feature discussed in Chapter 2 relied on code generators that used this technique.

Usually, though, you won't be too interested in the database columns behind your model—you'll want to use attributes instead. For each column in the database, Rails creates an attribute. In fact, you've already seen that you can access the database column data of a photo through its attribute, `photo.filename`, for example. The Rails implementation isn't necessarily what you'd expect. Experienced Ruby programmers might expect to see an accessor for `filename` as a method on `photo`. An accessor is a simple method that's used to access an attribute.

Active Record uses a Ruby metaprogramming trick to attach custom finders. It overrides the `method_missing` method. The `method_missing` technique involves overriding the Ruby method that the interpreter invokes any time you call a method that is not found. Active Record overrides `method_missing` to add accessor methods that make it easy to access the custom finders such as `find_by_filename`. If you ever wanted to use the technique yourself, it would look something like this:

```
class Talker
  def method_missing(method)
    puts method.to_s.sub('say_', '') if method.to_s =~ /say_/
  end
end
```

This `Talker` class responds to any method name beginning with `say_`, even though no method beginning with `say_` exists. The method simply prints the method name minus `say_`. For example, `Talker.new.say_hello` prints `hello`. Remember, an accessor method in Ruby returns the value of an attribute. Active Record uses `method_missing` to implement accessors so you can type `photo.find_by_filename('cat.jpg')`.

Identifiers

`id` is a special Active Record attribute that is the primary key for the database table. Our migration automatically created the `id` column and a primary key based on the `id`. The underlying table definition, shown in Figure 3-1, identifies the primary key with the `primary key(id)` statement. Table 3-1 shows the metaprogramming methods added to each Active Record class.

Table 3-1. Active Record adds these methods and attributes to model objects at runtime

Features	Purpose
Methods	
find_by_<column_name>	Active Record adds a class method to the class for each column in the database, including id. For example, Active Record adds find_by_id, find_by_name, and find_by_email to a class wrapping a table having id, name, and email columns.
find_by_<column_name>_and_<column_name>	Active Record also adds finders that combine groups of attributes. For example, a Person class wrapping a table with name and email columns would support Person.find_by_name_and_email(name, email).
Attributes	
<column_name>	Active Record creates an attribute with getters and setters for each property in the database. For example, photo.filename = "dog.jpg" would be legal for a photo instance of a class wrapping a table with a filename column.

Complex Classes

For Photo Share, we've built an object model in which one table relates to one class. Sometimes you'll want to map more sophisticated object models to a database table. The two most common scenarios for doing so are inheritance and composition. Let's look at how you'd handle each mapping with Active Record. These examples are not part of our Photo Share application, but the problems are common enough that we will show them to you here.

Inheritance

Active Record supports inheritance relationships using a strategy called *single-table inheritance*, shown in Figure 3-1. With this kind of inheritance mapping, all descendants of a common class use the same table. For example, a photographer is a person with a camera. With single-table inheritance, all columns for both Person and Photographer go into the same table. Consider the table created by this migration:

```
$ script/generate model person
      exists  app/models/
      exists  test/unit/
      exists  test/fixtures/
      create  app/models/person.rb
      create  test/unit/person_test.rb
      create  test/fixtures/people.yml
      exists  db/migrate
      create  db/migrate/20080510174956_create_people.rb
```

As usual, you can edit the migration in db/migrate/20080510174956_create_people.rb:

```
class CreatePeople < ActiveRecord::Migration
  def self.up
    create_table :people do |t|
      t.string :name, :type, :email, :camera
      t.timestamps
    end
  end

  def self.down
    drop_table :people
  end
end
```

Next, run the migration:

```
rake db:migrate
(in /Users/lancelotcarlson/Projects/book/repo/current/src/chapter3/photos)
== 20080510174956 CreatePeople: migrating ======================================
-- create_table(:people)
   -> 0.0038s
== 20080510174956 CreatePeople: migrated (0.0040s) =============================
```

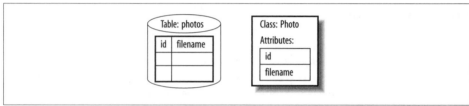

Figure 3-1. Rails supports single-table inheritance between an entity (Person) and a subclass (Photographer)

Now, we need classes, which are trivial:

```
class Photographer < Person
end
```

A query against **Person** will return **people** and **photographers**. Active Record doesn't need to build any special support to handle a query against a superclass. Subclasses are more difficult. In order to allow a query returning only **Photographers**, Active Record must have some way to determine the type of an object for an individual row. Active Record uses the **type** field for this purpose.

Notice that we declared **Photographer** as a subclass of **Person**. Active Record will manage the **type** attribute for you. You'll be able to access the **camera** property from **Photographer**. You can see the usage of the classes in the console:

```
$ script/console
>> Photographer
=> Photographer(id: integer, name: string, type: string, email: string, camera: string,
created_at: datetime, updated_at: datetime)
>> Photographer.new[:type]
=> "Photographer"
```

```
>> Person.create :name => 'bruce', :email => 'b@t.com'
=> #<Person id: 1, name: "bruce", type: nil, email: "b@t.com", camera: nil,
created_at: "2008-05-10 13:36:35", updated_at: "2008-05-10 13:36:35">
>> Photographer.create :name => 'lance', :email => 'l@c.com', :camera => 'iphone'
=> #<Photographer id: 2, name: "lance",
type: "Photographer", email: "l@c.com", camera: "iphone",
created_at: "2008-05-10 13:37:27", updated_at: "2008-05-10 13:37:27">
>> Photographer.count
=> 1
>> Person.count
=> 2
>> Person.find_by_name('bruce').camera
=> nil
>> Person.find_by_name('lance').camera
=> "iphone"
```

Active Record's implementation of inheritance is not exactly true inheritance. With Active Record's inheritance, all items in an inheritance tree have the same attributes. For example, in our model, all people have cameras even though they are not photographers. With a purer implementation of inheritance, only photographers would have cameras. In practice, that limitation is a compromise, and not a bad one for most uses of inheritance. A parent can usually simply ignore attributes introduced by subclasses. You get slightly better performance for most situations, because fewer tables means fewer joins. You also get a simpler schema because you only have a single table to worry about. The trade-off is that this inheritance strategy is not flexible or powerful enough to handle the most demanding situations. For example, if all of your model objects were to inherit from a common base class, all of your model classes would pull data from the same gigantic table!

 Normally, only Active Record needs to set the **type** attribute. Be careful when you need to manage **type** yourself. You can't say **person.type** because **type** is a class method on the base Ruby class called **Object**. If you need to see the value of the **type** field, use **person[:type]** instead.

Composition

If you want to extend a **Person** class with **Address**, you would normally use a **has_one** relationship or a **belongs_to** relationship. That solution only works if you want to keep your **Address** columns in a table separate from your **Person** columns. To point two objects to the same table, you need to use composition. Composition works well when you want to use a pervasive type like address or currency across many Active Record models, and the supporting columns are repeated across your database schema. You'll use **composed_of** for this type of relationship, as shown in Figure 3-2.

Let's look at a **Person** that is **composed_of** an **Address**. In a composition relationship, there's a main class (**Person**) and one or more component classes (**Address**). Each component class explicitly references one or more database columns. Generate a migration by typing **script/generate migration add_address_to_person**.

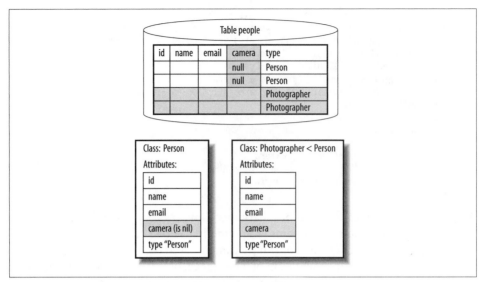

Figure 3-2. Composed_of maps many objects onto one table

```
$ script/generate migration add_address_to_person
      exists  db/migrate
      create  db/migrate/20080510175651_add_address_to_person.rb
```

Now that you have a migration template, you can edit the migration code in *db/migrate/20080510175651_add_address_to_person.rb* (remember, your timestamp could be different):

```ruby
class AddAddressToPerson < ActiveRecord::Migration
  def self.up
    add_column :people, :street_address, :string
    add_column :people, :city, :string
    add_column :people, :state, :string
    add_column :people, :zip, :string
  end

  def self.down
    remove_column :people, :street_address
    remove_column :people, :city
    remove_column :people, :state
    remove_column :people, :zip
  end
end
```

Run the migration with `rake db:migrate`:

```
$ rake db:migrate
(in /Users/lancelotcarlson/Projects/book/repo/current/src/chapter3/photos)
== 20080510175651 AddAddressToPerson: migrating ================================
-- add_column(:people, :street_address, :string)
   -> 0.0121s
-- add_column(:people, :city, :string)
   -> 0.0105s
```

```
-- add_column(:people, :state, :string)
   -> 0.0116s
-- add_column(:people, :zip, :string)
   -> 0.0169s
== 20080510175651 AddAddressToPerson: migrated (0.0520s) =====================
```

Now you have a working schema with one table with the columns for a person and an address. Your goal is to manage rows in the people table with two classes: Person and Address. Edit your Person class (in *app/models/person.rb*) and create *app/models/address.rb* file to look like the following classes:

```
app/models/person.rb
class Person < ActiveRecord::Base
  composed_of :address, :class_name => "Address",
              :mapping => [%w(street_address street_address),
                           %w(city city),
                           %w(state state),
                           %w(zip zip)]
end

app/models/address.rb
class Address
  attr_reader :street_address, :city, :state, :zip

  def initialize(street_address, city, state, zip)
    @street_address = street_address
    @city = city
    @state = state
    @zip = zip
  end
end
```

We've been explicit here, but if the first parameter for composed_of and the name of the component class are the same, Active Record can infer the name of the component class. Otherwise, you can override it with a :class_name modifier. Notice that only Person is an Active Record class. Address is a pure Ruby class, one that the Person class will manage.

In Rails terminology, Address is the component class. For each database column that the component represents, the component class must have an attribute and a parameter in the initialize method. In the mapping section, you see the attribute name from the Active Record object followed by the name of the accessor in the component object.

Now when you use Person, you will have an address property that is an address. Break open the console or reload it if you've already got it open and play with your new model:

```
>> reload!
Reloading...
=> true
>> address = Address.new('3734 Elvis Presley Boulevard', 'Memphis', 'Tn', '38186')
=> #<Address:0x22be754 @street_address="3734 Elvis Presley Boulevard",
@zip="38186", @state="Tn", @city="Memphis">
>> Person.create(:name => 'Elvis', :address => address)
=> #<Person id: 3, name: "Elvis", type: nil, email: nil, camera: nil,
```

```
created_at: "2008-05-10 15:05:33", updated_at: "2008-05-10 15:05:33",
street_address: "3734 Elvis Presley Boulevard",
city: "Memphis", state: "Tn", zip: "38186">
>> Person.find_by_name('Elvis').address.city
=> "Memphis"
```

Though `street_address`, `city`, `state`, and `zip` are columns on the `people` table, you don't use those attributes on any `Person` object directly. Instead, access these attributes through the `address` attribute on `Person`. Table 3-2 shows the attributes added by a `composed_of` relationship.

Table 3-2. Metaprogramming for composed_of :class

Attributes	Description
`<class>`	The component class (`person.address`)
`<class>_<attribute>`	Attributes for the component class (`person.address_zip`)

Behavior

The core Active Record design pattern relies on making CRUD operations available on classes and instances. If you want to work with data from a table, use the class. Methods such as `find` and `count` work on a class. If you want to work with a table row, use an instance. Methods such as `save`, `update`, and `destroy` work on instances. `ActiveRecord::Base` class supplies many of the methods, and `method_missing` provides most of the rest. You can find the documentation for the latest stable Active Record version online at the following address: *http://api.rubyonrails.com*.

Finders

Whenever you need to find instances of some type, you will use one of the many forms of finders. The most basic form is `ClassName.find(id)`. The `id` is an identifier of the instance you need to find. In place of the identifier, you can use `:all` to find all instances, or `:first` to find only the first instance. Finders have many options. You can specify the options after the id field in a hash map. Remember, in Ruby, you can omit the braces in your hash map if the hash is the last parameter in your method. You'll often see Rails developers do this. We'll walk you through a few of these in Table 3-3, and also in the console.

Table 3-3. Rails finder options

Option	Description
`conditions`	*:conditions => ["name = ?", name]*. Specify conditions in the form of a SQL where clause. If you have input parameters, you can pass an array, where the first element is the condition string and the following elements are the replacement parameters.
`limit`	*:limit => 50*. Specify the maximum number of rows returned by Active Record.
`offset`	*:offset => page * PAGE_SIZE*. Skip this number of rows from the result set. This option is useful for paging.

Option	Description
order	*:order => 'updated_at desc'*. Specify the order of columns in the form of a SQL `order` statement.
select	*:select => 'id, name, email'*. Specify the columns to be returned by the query. This option is useful for performance, and also to create temporary attributes that your model can use. Be careful—if you don't include an attribute in your `select`, you can't use it in your code.

Other `find` options are available as well, but most of those relate to working with relationships. We'll cover them later in the book. For now, use your console to play with some of these options:

```
>> Photo.find(1)
=> #<Photo id: 1, ...>
>> Photo.find(:first)
=> #<Photo id: 1, ...>
>> Photo.find(:all)
=> [#<Photo id: 1, ...>, #<Photo id: 2, ...>, #<Photo id: 3, ...>,
#<Photo id: 4, ...>, #<Photo id: 5, ...>, #<Photo id: 6, ...>,
#<Photo id: 7, ...>, #<Photo id: 8, ...>, #<Photo id: 9, ...>]
>> Photo.find(:all, :limit => 2)
=> [#<Photo id: 1, ...>, #<Photo id: 2, ...>]
>> Photo.find(:all, :limit => 2, :offset => 1)
=> [#<Photo id: 2, ...>, #<Photo id: 3, ...>]
>> Photo.find(:all, :order => 'filename')
=> [#<Photo id: 9, filename: "baskets.jpg", thumbnail: "baskets_t.jpg", ...>,
#<Photo id: 8, filename: "bear.jpg", thumbnail: "bear_t.jpg", ...>, ...]
```

Now that we've seen the basic finders in action, we should cover a few more useful kinds of finders. `find_by_sql` lets you type SQL directly into a finder, and your objects will have the attributes for the columns that the query returns. But watch out—you can get some pretty strange results if you're not careful. Try these finders in your console. Notice that the last allows you to load **people** data from the **photos** table:

```
>> Photo.find_by_sql("select * from photos")
=> [#<Photo id: 1, filename: "train.jpg", thumbnail: "train_t.jpg", ...>,
#<Photo id: 2, filename: "lighthouse.jpg", ...]
>> photos = Photo.find_by_sql("select * from people")
=> [#<Photo id: 1, ...>]
>> photos[0].email
=> "b@t.com"
```

You can also use custom finders that have the form `find_by_<column_name>` on any model class for each column in that model's table. You can also string together column names with `_and_`, so you can use any finder of the form `find_by_<column_name>_and_<another_column_name>`! That's an amazing amount of default behavior.

```
>> Photo.find_by_id(1)
=> #<Photo id: 1, filename: "train.jpg", thumbnail: "train_t.jpg",
description: "A park I've never been to", ...>
>> Photo.find_by_filename("train.jpg")
=> #<Photo id: 1, filename: "train.jpg", thumbnail: "train_t.jpg",
description: "A park I've never been to", ...>
```

```
>> Photo.find_by_id_and_filename(1, "train.jpg")
=> #<Photo id: 1, filename: "train.jpg", thumbnail: "train_t.jpg",
description: "A park I've never been to", ...>
```

You can also use Active Record to save, update, and delete objects. The **save** method comes in two forms: **save** and **save!**. Both will save all changes that you make to the target object. If the command fails, **save** will return **false**, and **save!** will return a **RecordNotSaved** exception. You've already seen the **save** command in use.

Active Record supports two forms of update. **update_attribute** will update the value of a single attribute. Finally, **update_attributes** takes a hash map as a parameter, and updates all of the attributes named by the keys in the hash map with the corresponding values. Try it in the console:

```
>> reload!
Reloading...
=> true
>> photo = Photo.find(1)
=> #<Photo id: 1, filename: "balboa_park.jpg", thumbnail: "balboa_park_thumb.jpg",
description: "A park I've never been to", ...>
>> photo.update_attribute(:filename, 'updated_train.jpg')
=> true
>> photo.filename
=> "updated_train.jpg"
>> Person.find(1).update_attributes(:name => 'Elvis Presley',
:email => 'jelly@donut.com')
=> true
>> Person.find(1).email
=> "jelly@donut.com"
>> Person.find(1).name
=> "Elvis Presley"
```

We've marched through create, read, and update from CRUD. Only delete remains. You have two methods at your disposal: **delete** and **destroy**, which do slightly different things. **delete** aborts on minor errors, but **destroy** does not abort unless there's a critical database error. You can also update objects. As usual, use the console to try it out:

```
>> person = Person.find(1)
=> #<Person id: 1, name: "Elvis Presley", type: nil, email: "jelly@donut.com",
camera: nil, created_at: "2008-05-21 02:09:02", updated_at:
"2008-05-21 02:12:53", street_address: nil, city: nil, state: nil,
zip: nil>
>> person.destroy
=> #<Person id: 1, name: "Elvis Presley", type: nil, email: "jelly@donut.com",
camera: nil, created_at: "2008-05-21 02:09:02", updated_at:
"2008-05-21 02:12:53", street_address: nil, city: nil, state: nil,
zip: nil>
>> Person.find(1)
ActiveRecord::RecordNotFound: Couldn't find Person with ID=1
    from /Users/lancelotcarlson/Projects/book/repo/current/src/chapter5/photos/
vendor/rails/activerecord/lib/active_record/base.rb:1352:in `find_one'
    from /Users/lancelotcarlson/Projects/book/repo/current/src/chapter5/photos/
vendor/rails/activerecord/lib/active_record/base.rb:1335:in `find_from_ids'
    from /Users/lancelotcarlson/Projects/book/repo/current/src/chapter5/photos/
```

```
vendor/rails/activerecord/lib/active_record/base.rb:519:in `find'
    from (irb):3
```

Beginning with Rails 2.1, Active Record adds a feature called named_scope. Based on a popular plug-in called has_finder, named_scope essentially lets you declare a method that will behave like a new model that meets your conditions. It's easier to show than to explain. All you need to do to specify one finder that selects all jpeg images, and another that weeds out photos without thumbnails, is add the following code to *app/model/photo.rb*:

```
class Photo < ActiveRecord::Base
  named_scope :with_filetype_jpg, :conditions => "filename like '%.jpg'"
  named_scope :with_thumbnail, :conditions => "thumbnail not null and thumbnail != ''"
end
```

When you put the features through their paces, you will notice that you can stack the named scopes as deeply as you would like:

```
>> reload!
Reloading...
=> true
>> Photo.with_filetype_jpg
=> [#<Photo id: 1, filename: "updated_train.jpg", thumbnail: "train_t.jpg",
 description: "A park I've never been to", created_at: "2008-05-21 02:07:29",
   updated_at: "2008-05-21 02:12:22">, ...]
>> Photo.with_filetype_jpg.count
=> 12
>> Photo.with_filetype_jpg.with_thumbnail
=> [#<Photo id: 1, filename: "updated_train.jpg", thumbnail: "train_t.jpg",
 description: "A park I've never been to", created_at: "2008-05-21 02:07:29",
   updated_at: "2008-05-21 02:12:22">, ...]
>> Photo.with_filetype_jpg.with_thumbnail.count
=> 9
>> Photo.with_filetype_jpg.with_thumbnail.find(5)
=> #<Photo id: 5, filename: "cappucino.jpg", thumbnail: "cappucino_t.jpg",
 description: "Ruby on trains?", created_at: "2008-05-21 02:07:29",
   updated_at: "2008-05-21 02:07:29">
```

If you wish, you can easily provide a parameter to the with_filetype named scope, so you can plug in any file type you'd like. The syntax uses an old Lisp term called a lambda expression, but it's not too hard to follow:

```
named_scope :with_filetype,
    lambda {|ftype| {:conditions => ["filename like ?", "%.#{ftype}"] } }
```

The lambda expression is used to capture the code block. The code block takes a parameter and specifies a code block that will execute when you trigger the named scope. The new syntax looks like this:

```
>> reload!
Reloading...
=> true
>> Photo.with_filetype('jpg')
=> [#<Photo id: 1, filename: "updated_train.jpg", thumbnail: "train_t.jpg",
```

```
description: "A park I've never been to", created_at: "2008-05-21 02:07:29",
updated_at: "2008-05-21 02:12:22">, ...]
```

Those commands complete the tour of the basic CRUD methods for Active Record
instances. In the next section, you'll see some advanced functionality: built-in conver-
sations and validation.

Validation

So far, you've used Active Record to do database operations on an object. You can also
use Active Record for simple validation. For example, you can verify that the
filename property exists with one line of code. Change the Photo class in
app/models/photo.rb to look like this:

```
class Photo < ActiveRecord::Base
  validates_presence_of :filename
  named_scope :with_filetype_jpg, :conditions => "filename like '%.jpg'"
  named_scope :with_thumbnail, :conditions => "thumbnail not null and thumbnail != ''"
  named_scope :with_filetype,
    lambda {|ftype| {:conditions => ["filename like ?", "%.#{ftype}"] } }
end
```

Let's see how the validation works. Go back to the console (don't forget to reload!),
and try to save a blank photo:

```
>> photo = Photo.new
=> #<Photo:0x3501b70 @attributes={"filename"=>""}, @new_record=true>
>> photo.save
=> false
```

The save failed. (If it didn't, you forgot to reload!) Let's find out why it failed:

```
>> photo.errors.each {|attribute, error| puts attribute + ": " +error}
filename: can't be blank
=> {"filename"=>["can't be blank"]}
```

The validation saved a hash map of errors. For each attribute, there's an array of errors.
You will later use these error messages as you build your user interfaces to display
validation errors. You can do several different kinds of validation, or you can create
your own. You could validate an email message like this:

```
validates_format_of :email,
                    :with => /^([^@\s]+)@((?:[-a-z0-9]+\.)+[a-z]{2,})$/i
```

Or, you could validate the length of a field like this:

```
validates_length_of :name, :within => 6..100
```

Later, you'll see that the Rails view integration uses this information to present mean-
ingful error messages; look for those details in Chapter 5. You've seen the basics of
working with Active Record classes. You use a model object or its class to directly
manipulate rows in the database table. Active Record goes beyond most traditional

wrapping frameworks because it helps you manage relationships between tables. In the next few sections, let's look into how Active Record manages simple relationships.

Transactions

Photo Share doesn't require transactions, but for many applications, transactional behavior is critical. If you have some code that must be executed as a single unit, you can use Active Record transactions. The most common example is a transfer between two accounts. A transfer is fundamentally a debit and a credit. The Ruby code for a transfer between the from and to Active Record Account models might look like this:

```
def transfer(from, to, amount)
  from.debit(amount)
  to.credit(amount)
end
```

You wouldn't want this method to fail after the debit—if it did, the holder of the from account would be shorted by amount. So, you use a transaction. This is the way it works:

```
def transfer(from, to, amount)
  Account.transaction do
    from.debit(amount)
    to.credit(amount)
  end
end
```

transaction is a method on all Active Record classes. With this approach, you can maintain the integrity of your transactions.

Conversions

One of our favorite Active Record features is the built-in conversions. You can quickly convert an object to XML or even JSON. Both are useful when you're building dynamic websites using a technique called Ajax. Using the feature is marvelously simple. You just call one of the to_xml, to_yaml, or to_json methods. Try it now:

```
>> photo = Photo.find(2)
=> #<Photo id: 2, filename: "lighthouse.jpg", thumbnail: "lighthouse_t.jpg",
description: "My ride to work", created_at: "2008-05-21 02:07:29",
updated_at: "2008-05-21 02:07:29">
>> puts photo.to_xml
<?xml version="1.0" encoding="UTF-8"?>
<photo>
  <created-at type="datetime">2008-05-21T02:07:29-04:00</created-at>
  <description>My ride to work</description>
  <filename>lighthouse.jpg</filename>
  <id type="integer">2</id>
  <thumbnail>lighthouse_t.jpg</thumbnail>
  <updated-at type="datetime">2008-05-21T02:07:29-04:00</updated-at>
</photo>
=> nil
```

```
>> puts photo.to_yaml
--- !ruby/object:Photo
attributes:
  thumbnail: lighthouse_t.jpg
  updated_at: 2008-05-21 02:07:29
  id: "2"
  description: My ride to work
  filename: lighthouse.jpg
  created_at: 2008-05-21 02:07:29
attributes_cache:
  updated_at: 2008-05-21 02:07:29 -04:00
  created_at: 2008-05-21 02:07:29 -04:00
=> nil
>> puts photo.to_json
{"updated_at": "2008/05/21 02:07:29 -0400", "thumbnail": "lighthouse_t.jpg",
"id": 2, "description": "My ride to work", "filename": "lighthouse.jpg",
"created_at": "2008/05/21 02:07:29 -0400"}
```

Moving Forward

In the next chapter, we'll look at managing relationships between Active Record classes. We'll see most types of Active Record relationships in action, including:

- belongs_to
- has_one
- has_many
- has_and_belongs_to_many
- acts_as_list
- acts_as_tree

We'll build each of these into our evolving Photo Share object model, including the base relationships has_one, has_many, and has_and_belongs_to_many, as well as the plug-ins acts_as_list and acts_as_tree. By the end of the next chapter, we'll have a fully functioning, database-backed object model.

## CHAPTER 4

Active Record Relationships

You've seen how Active Record treats a model backed by a single table. You wrote very little code, and got impressive behavior for free. But Photo Share will need many different models working together. In this chapter, you'll learn how to deal with relationships. Active Record takes advantage of the Ruby language and naming conventions to simplify the way you work with related tables through related models.

In Chapter 3, you got a taste of Active Record's language for relationships and validations. Adding the macro `validates_presence_of :filename` record to the class added all of the code that your class needed to support validation. You'll deal with relationships the same way. Rather than adding a bunch of methods and attributes to your class explicitly to manage a foreign key relationship, you'll describe the relationship using a little bit of syntax called a macro and let Active Record do the rest. Rails will add everything you need to manage each relationship based on a few short lines of code.

You'll specify a relationship, also called an association, in three parts: the relationship macro, the association or target, and an optional hash of additional parameters. For example, this code:

```
class Slideshow < ActiveRecord::Base
  has_many :slides, :order => 'position'
```

specifies that a single `Slideshow` `has_many` `:slides`, and they are ordered by the position attribute. The macro is `has_many`, the association is `:slides`, and the hash of options is `{:order => 'position'}`.

Let's add relationships to the existing `Photo`, `Slide`, `Slideshow`, and `Category` classes. If you haven't already done so, and you want to start coding your way through the book with us, copy your code from *http://www.oreilly.com/catalog/9780596522001*, using the file for Chapter 3. Run `rake photos:reset` to run your migrations and reset your test data. Now you're ready to follow along.

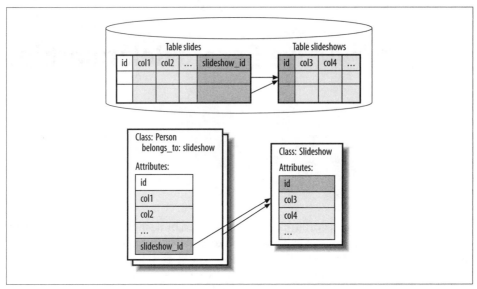

Figure 4-1. belongs_to :association relationship between entity (slide) and association (slideshow)

Relational Database Relationships

Relational databases are fundamentally based on different kinds of relationships between tables. A set of table columns called *keys* provides the structure for all relationships. A *primary key* is a set of columns in a table that uniquely identify a row within that same table. A *foreign key* is a set of columns in a table that uniquely identifies a row in another table. A database manager can *join* two tables by matching the primary keys in one table to the foreign keys in another. Active Record also uses primary and foreign keys to manage relationships. As of this writing, Active Record limits its primary keys to a single database column. Unless the Rails team builds in composite keys, you'll need to install a third-party plug-in to handle any schema that requires a multicolumn key.

belongs_to

The most common database relationship is many-to-one. Figure 4-1 shows how Active Record maps the "many" side of such a relationship. In Photo Share, we want users to be able to build slideshows. A slideshow contains an ordered list of pictures. We can't simply use pictures in a slideshow because a picture has no way of keeping its position in a slideshow, so we'll introduce a `Slide` class. We'll then need a many-to-one relationship between slides and slideshows because a slideshow consists of many slides, but each slide (a photo combined with a position) can belong to only one slideshow. A slide also belongs to a photo. We'll implement both relationships with `belongs_to`.

You've already generated a model and migration for Slide, and another for Slideshow. You can open up *db/schema.rb* to verify that your Photos schema has a table called slides and another called photos. Notice that the slide has a slideshow_id and a photo_id. Any model that uses belongs_to must be backed by a table that has the supporting foreign key. Next, modify the Slide model in *app/models/slide.rb*, adding the two relationships:

```
class Slide < ActiveRecord::Base
  belongs_to :slideshow
  belongs_to :photo
end
```

That's it. You have two working belongs_to relationships. Verify them briefly in the console. (Remember, you can start the console with ruby script/console, or simply use reload! to reload it whenever your models change.)

```
>> slide = Slide.new
=> #<Slide id: nil, position: nil, photo_id: nil, slideshow_id: nil,
created_at: nil, updated_at: nil>
>> slide.create_slideshow
=> #<Slideshow id: 2, name: nil, created_at: "2008-05-10 17:45:46",
updated_at: "2008-05-10 17:45:46">
>> slide.photo = Photo.find(2)
=> #<Photo id: 2, filename: "lighthouse.jpg", thumbnail: "lighthouse_t.jpg",
description: "My ride to work", created_at: "2008-05-21 02:07:29",
updated_at: "2008-05-21 02:07:29">
>> slide.photo.filename
=> "lighthouse.jpg"
>> slide.slideshow.id
=> 2
```

You can see the belongs_to relationship at work. You have at least two new attributes: slideshow and photo. You also have the create_slideshow and create_photo methods. These methods are only the tip of the iceberg. Table 4-1 shows all of the methods and attributes introduced by the belongs_to macro.

Table 4-1. Metaprogramming for belongs_to and has_one

Added Feature	Description
Methods	
<association>.nil?	Test the association for a nil value: slide.photo.nil?
build_<association>	Build an object of the associated type, but do not save it yet: slide.build_photo(:filename => "cat.jpg").
	In this example, slide.photo is initialized to a new unsaved photo with the specified attributes.
create_<association>	Create and save an object of the associated type, initialized to the root object. It takes a hash map of attributes for the new object as a parameter: slideshow.create_slide({...}).

Added Feature	Description
Attributes	
`<association>`	An attribute of the type of the associated object: `belongs_to :photo` on `Slide` allows `slide.photo` and `slide.photo = nil`

As you can see, just learning the macros isn't enough. To learn about using Active Record to the fullest, you need to understand all of the methods and attributes that `belongs_to` creates for you. You'll find the association attribute and the constructors—all forms of build and create methods—particularly useful. We'll show you tables such as Table 4-1 for each macro we cover.

In the meantime, let's take another look at the new models in the Rails console:

```
>> slide = Slide.find 1
=> #<Slide id: 1, position: 1, photo_id: 1, slideshow_id: 1,
created_at: "2008-05-10 17:45:34",
updated_at: "2008-05-10 17:45:34">
>> slide.photo.filename
=> "train.jpg"
>> slide.slideshow.name
=> "Interesting Pictures"
```

`belongs_to` is only the "many" end of a many-to-one relationship. Let's look at the "one" side.

has_many

Now that you've finished the relationships on `Slide`, you'll need to implement `has_many` relationships on `Photo` and `Slideshow`. Figure 4-2 shows the mapping between Active Record objects and database tables with `has_many`.

`has_many` is the other side of a `belongs_to` relationship. Both models and the schema exist, so you don't need to modify the class or table for `Slide`. You can merely add the relationship `has_many` to *slideshow.rb* in *app/models/slideshow.rb*:

```
class Slideshow < ActiveRecord::Base
  has_many :slides
end
```

You'll do the same to *app/models/photo.rb*:

```
class Photo < ActiveRecord::Base
...
  has_many :slides
  validates_presence_of :filename
...
end
```

We should explain a little bit about the model. A slide belongs to a photo, but a photo has many slides. With this design, you give users the ability to use the same photo in

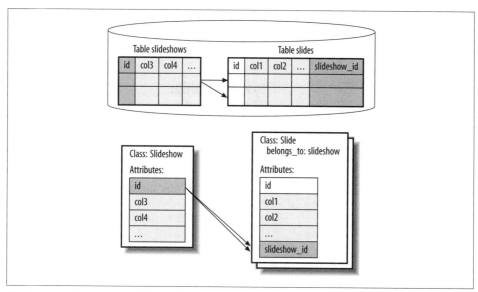

Figure 4-2. The entity (slideshow) has_many :associations (slides) relationship is a one-to-many relationship

several different slideshows. Remember: a slide is a photo and a position in a specific slideshow. So, a slide can't be reused, but a photo can.

With those code changes, you can see all of the slides associated with a photo and all of the slides in a slideshow. As usual, you can open the console to see the model in action:

```
>> reload!
Reloading...
=> true
>> slide = Slide.find 1
=> #<Slide id: 1, position: 1, photo_id: 1, slideshow_id: 1,
created_at: "2008-05-10 17:45:34", updated_at: "2008-05-10 17:45:34">
>> slideshow = slide.slideshow
=> #<Slideshow id: 1, name: "Interesting Pictures", created_at: "2008-05-10 17:45:34",
updated_at: "2008-05-10 17:45:34">
>> slideshow.slides.each {|s| puts s.photo.filename}
train.jpg
lighthouse.jpg
gargoyle.jpg
cat.jpg
cappucino.jpg
building.jpg
bridge.jpg
bear.jpg
baskets.jpg
=> [#<Slide id: 1, ...]
```

So, you get a list of slides in the slideshow, and each has an associated photo. Active Record is now managing the has_many relationship between Slideshow and Slide. You could use `photo.slides` in the same way. Table 4-2 shows you the metaprogramming for `has_many`.

Cascading Relationships

Many-to-one relationships introduce some problems for persistence frameworks. Primarily, the framework designer has to decide whether deleting a parent object also deletes child objects. Automatic deletion of dependent objects is called *cascading deletes*. Sometimes, you want automatic deletion to happen. For example, deleting an invoice should also delete the line items for that invoice. But sometimes, you want related objects to stay: employees should not be deleted when a department is dissolved. If you define a relationship with the `:dependent` option, deleting a row also deletes the associated objects. For example, to define an invoice, you might specify your invoice like this:

```
class Invoice < ActiveRecord::Base
  has_many :line_items, :dependent => :destroy
end
```

With this definition, deleting an invoice would also delete associated line items, each with a separate query. Sometimes, using a separate query to delete each child is unnecessarily inefficient, but there's a remedy. If the line items belong to one invoice—and only one—you can set the `:dependent => :delete_all` option on has_many, and Active Record will delete all dependent objects with one query.

Similarly, when you *read* an object, you need to decide whether to load dependent objects. By default, Active Record does not cascade loads. But you can load children when you load a parent by using the `:include` option on any finder.

Table 4-2. Metaprogramming for has_many

Added feature	Description
Methods	
`<associations> << object`	Adds an object to the `<associations>` collection: `photo.slides << a_slide`
`<associations>.delete object`	Deletes an object in the `<associations>` collection. The objects will be destroyed if the dependent parameter of has_many is set to `true`: `photo.slides.delete a_slide`
`<associations>_singular_ids collection`	Replaces the `<associations>` collection with a collection of objects identified by `ids` in the collection: `photo.slides_singular_ids [1, 2, 3, 4]`
`<associations>.find`	Uses the same rules as a basic find, but operates only on the items in the `<associations>` collection: `photo.slides.find_by_position 4`
`<associations>.clear`	Deletes all of the objects in the association: `photo.slides.clear`

Added feature	Description
`<associations>.empty?`	Tests to see if `<associations>` collection is empty: `photo.slides.clear` *empty?*
`<associations>.size`	Returns the number of items in the `<associations>` collection: `photo.slides.size`
`<associations>.build`	Builds an object of the associated type without saving it. It takes a hash map of attributes for the new object as a parameter: `slide.build_photo(:filename => "cat.jpg")`
`<associations>.create`	Creates and save an object of the associated type, initialized to the root object. It takes a hash map of attributes for the new object as a parameter: `slide.build_photo(:filename => "cat.jpg")` In this example, `photo.slide` is initialized to `slide`.
Attributes	
`<associations>`	A collection of the associated objects: `slide.photos[4]`

has_one

The simplest database relationship is the one-to-one relationship. With Active Record, you can implement one-to-one relationships with `belongs_to` or `has_one`. You'll decide which to use based on where the foreign key lands. For example, if an `Address` belonged to a `Person`, the `addresses` table would need a `person_id` column. `Person` would use a `has_one` relationship. Figure 4-3 shows a `has_one` relationship.

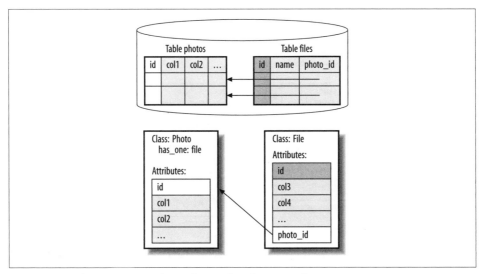

Figure 4-3. In this one-to-one relationship, a Photo has_one File

Let's take a simple example. Hypothetically, you could have decided to implement photos and files in separate tables. If you put a foreign key called `photo_id` into the `files` table, you would have this Active Record Photo class:

```
class Photo < ActiveRecord::Base
  has_one :file
  ...
end
```

`has_one` is identical to `belongs_to` with respect to metaprogramming. For example, adding `has_one :photo` or `belongs_to :photo` to `Slide` would add the `photo` attribute to `Slide`. But the Photo Share application does not need a separate table to manage files, so let's move on to that marathon of typing, `has_and_belongs_to_many`.

has_and_belongs_to_many

Many-to-many relationships are more complex than the three relationships shown so far because these relationships require an additional table in the database. Rather than relying on a single foreign key column, you'll need a *relationship table*, also called a *join table*. Each row of a join table expresses a relationship with foreign keys, but has no other data. Figure 4-4 shows our relationship table.

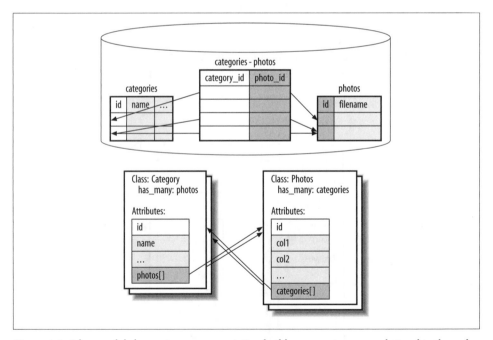

Figure 4-4. A has_and_belongs_to_many association builds a many-to-many relationship through a join table

Photo Share requires a many-to-many relationship between Photo and Category. A category can hold many photos, and the same photo can fit into more than one category. Many-to-many relationships won't work with a single foreign key. You already have a working model for both Category and Photo, but this many-to-many relationship will require a join table to manage relationships between the two classes. By convention, the join table should have the foreign keys photo_id and category_id. Generate that table now:

```
$ script/generate migration create_categories_photos
      exists  db/migrate
      create  db/migrate/20080511031501_create_categories_photos.rb
```

The generator created a migration for you, but not a model. You don't need an additional model for a join table. The Active Record naming convention for the relationship table is classes1_classes2, with the classes in alphabetical order. Edit the migration in *db/migrate/20080511031501_create_categories_photos.rb* to look like this:

```
class CreateCategoriesPhotos < ActiveRecord::Migration
  def self.up
    create_table :categories_photos, :id => false do |t|
      t.integer    :category_id
      t.integer    :photo_id
    end
  end

  def self.down
    drop_table :categories_photos
  end
end
```

Run the migration with rake db:migrate. Note that the categories_photos statement has the option :id => false. We added this option because the database table needs no id, only the foreign keys to photos and categories. The *app/models/photo.rb* and *app/models/category.rb* models need the has_and_belongs_to_many relationship macro, like this:

```
class Photo < ActiveRecord::Base

  ...
  has_many :slides
  has_and_belongs_to_many :categories
  ...
```

Next, edit app/models/category.rb to look like this:

```
class Category < ActiveRecord::Base
  has_and_belongs_to_many :photos
end
```

The has_and_belongs_to_many macro works just like the other Active Record macros you've seen. It will add the appropriate attributes and constructors to the each class. To play with the class, you will need some test data for the categories. Create a fixture in *test/fixtures/categories_photos.yml* that looks like this:

```
<% 1.upto(9) do |i| %>
categories_photos_<%= i %>:
  category_id: 1
  photo_id: <%= i %>
<% end %>
```

Load your fixtures with rake db:fixtures:load, or run rake photos:reset to run migrations and load your test data. Now, you can see how categories are working inside the console with a richer set of data:

```
>> Photo.find(1).categories
=> [#<Category id: 1, parent_id: 1, name: "All",
created_at: "2008-05-11 00:37:27", updated_at: "2008-05-11 00:37:27">]
>> Category.count
=> 7
>> Category.find(1).photos.collect {|photo| photo.filename}.join ', '
=> "gargoyle.jpg, cat.jpg, cappucino.jpg, building.jpg, bridge.jpg,
bear.jpg, baskets.jpg, train.jpg, lighthouse.jpg"
>> all = Category.find(:first)
=> #<Category id: 1, parent_id: 1, name: "All",
created_at: "2008-05-11 00:37:27", updated_at: "2008-05-11 00:37:27">
```

As expected, you get an array called photos on category that's filled with photos associated in the join table categories_photos. Let's add a photo:

```
>> chunky_bacon = Photo.new(:filename => 'chunky_bacon.jpg')
=> #<Photo id: nil, filename: "chunky_bacon.jpg", thumbnail: nil, description: nil,
created_at: nil, updated_at: nil>
>> chunky_bacon.id
=> nil
>> all.photos << chunky_bacon
=> [#<Photo id: 3, filename: "gargoyle.jpg", ...]
>> chunky_bacon.id
=> 10
>> chunky_bacon.new_record?
=> false
```

Take a look at this statement: all.photos << chunky_bacon. (It adds a photo to all.photos.) You can see that the << operator adds an object to a collection and saves the collection. Because the initial chunky_bacon.id statement returns nil, you know that the object has not yet been saved. The << operator adds an object to a collection. As you know, the collection is represented in the database as two ids: one for the photo and one for the category. Active Record must save the record before adding it to a category to get the id. The behavior is a little jarring if you're not ready for it.

The methods and attributes added by the has_and_belongs_to_many method are identical to those added by has_many. They were shown in Table 4-2.

Join Models

Sometimes, it's useful to be able to add columns to a relationship table. You might wonder whether it's possible to create a Rails model from the categories_photos table.

You can't do so with the has_and_belongs_to_many macro in its basic form—you need join models and the through option. For example, we could have easily decided that a slide was just a join table between photo and slideshow with an attribute parameter. We could have expressed that relationship in this way:

```
class Slideshow < ActiveRecord::Base
  has_many :photos :through => :slides
end
```

This example relies on tables and models for photos, slideshows, and slides. The join table is a first-class model, but also serves as a relationship table. The structure in the example is slightly different from a typical join table. The primary differences are these:

- The Slide is a first-class model with an id.
- You can add attributes to Slide.
- You can use :through with has_many, belongs_to, and has_and_belongs_to_many.

The :through relationship makes it possible to build much more sophisticated relationships, allowing you to identify and tag each relationship with additional data as required.

acts_as_list

Active Record has three special relationships that let you explicitly model lists, trees, and nested sets: acts_as_list, acts_as_tree, and acts_as_nested_set, respectively. We'll look at the two relationships required by Photo Share in this chapter: acts_as_list and acts_as_tree. acts_as_list lets you express items as an ordered list and also provides methods to move items around in the hierarchy. Figure 4-5 shows the mapping. In Photo Share, we'll use acts_as_list to model a slideshow, which is an ordered list of slides. Later, we'll use acts_as_tree to manage our nested categories.

First, let's modify the existing *app/models/slide.rb* model. We want users to be able to move slides up and down in a show, so the slideshow needs an ordering. We'll use the existing slides and add the Active Record macro acts_as_list.

```
class Slide < ActiveRecord::Base
  belongs_to :slideshow
  belongs_to :photo

  acts_as_list :scope => "slideshow_id"
end
```

This example builds a list of slides that compose a slideshow. belongs_to is a one-to-many relationship, imposing structure. The Slide model has a belongs_to relationship with Slideshow and Photo as the targets. acts_as_list is a helper macro, imposing order and introducing behavior related to a list. As of Rails 2.0, the macro is a plug-in and not part of the base library. To get it, type: script/plugin install acts_as_list.

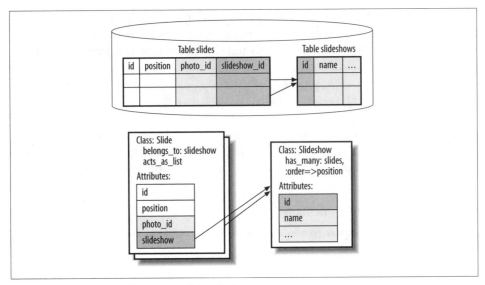

Figure 4-5. acts_as_list allows an explicit ordering

```
$ script/plugin install acts_as_list
+ ./README
+ ./init.rb
+ ./lib/active_record/acts/list.rb
+ ./test/list_test.rb
```

That command loads the `acts_as_list` plug-in into the *vendor/plugins/acts_as_list* directory. From that point, you can use it just as if it were a native Rails macro. To Active Record, each macro is independent. You use the `:scope` parameter to tell Active Record which items belong in the list. In this case, we set the `:scope` parameter to `:slide show_id` so all slides with the same `slideshow_id` will act as one independent list.

To capture ordering, Active Record uses a `position` attribute by default. Because you have a position column in the database, you don't need to do anything more to the slides to support this list. However, for convenience, you'll want the array of slides to be fetched and displayed in the right order, so make one small change to `app/models/slideshow.rb`:

```
class Slideshow < ActiveRecord::Base
  has_many :slides, :order => :position
end
```

We're ready to use the list. You can use methods added by `acts_as_list` to change the order of slides in the slideshow, and to indicate which items are first and last:

```
>> show = Slideshow.find 1
=> #<Slideshow id: 1, name: "Interesting Pictures", created_at: "2008-05-11 00:37:27",
updated_at: "2008-05-11 00:37:27">
>> show.slides.each {|slide| puts slide.photo.filename}
train.jpg
lighthouse.jpg
```

```
gargoyle.jpg
cat.jpg
cappucino.jpg
building.jpg
bridge.jpg
bear.jpg
baskets.jpg
=> [#<Slide id: 1, ...]
>> show.slides.first.photo.filename
=> "train.jpg"
>> show.slides.first.move_to_bottom
=> true
>> show.slides.last.photo.filename
=> "baskets.jpg"
>> show.reload
=> #<Slideshow id: 1, name: "Interesting Pictures", created_at: "2008-05-21 02:19:32",
updated_at: "2008-05-21 02:19:32">
>> show.slides
=> [#<Slide id: 2, ...>, ...]
>> show.slides.last.photo.filename
=> "train.jpg"
```

By convention, positions start at 1 and are sequentially numbered through the end of the list. Position 1 is the top, and the biggest number is the bottom. You can move any item higher or lower, move items to the top or bottom, create items in any position, and get relative items in the list, as in Table 4-3. Keep in mind that moving something higher means making the position smaller, so you should think of the position as a priority. Higher positions mean higher priorities, so they'll be closer to the front of the list.

Table 4-3 shows all the methods added by the `acts_as_list` relationship. Keep in mind that you'll use `acts_as_list` on objects that already have a `belongs_to` relationship, so you'll also get the methods and attributes provided by `belongs_to`. You'll also inherit the methods from the array, so `slideshow.slides[1]` and `slideshow.slides.first` are both legal.

Table 4-3. Metaprogramming features for acts_as_list

Added feature—methods	Description
increment_position	Increments the position attribute of this list element:
	`slideshow.slides[1].increment_position`
decrement_position	Decrements the position attribute of this list element:
	`slideshow.slides[2].decrement_position`
higher_item	Returns the previous item in the list. Higher means closer to the front, or closer to index 1, as in priority:
	`slideshow.slides[2].higher_item`
lower_item	Returns the next item in the list. Lower means closer to the back, or farther from index 1, as in priority:

Added feature—methods	Description
	`slideshow.slides[1].lower_item`
`in_list?`	Tests whether an object has been added to a list:
	`slide.in_list?`
`insert_at position`	Inserts the current item at a given position. Default is position 1:
	`slide.insert_at(1)`
`first?`	Returns true if `position==1`; false otherwise:
	`slide.first?`
`last?`	Returns true if position is the largest in the list; return `false` otherwise:
	`slideshow.slides[7].last?`
`move_higher`	Moves this item toward index 1:
	`slideshow.slides[4].move_lower`
`move_lower`	Moves this item away from index 1:
	`slideshow.slides[3].move_higher`
`move_to_top`	Moves this item to index 1:
	`slideshow.slides[3].move_to_top`
`move_to_bottom`	Makes this item the last in the list:
	`slideshow.slides[3].move_to_bottom`
`remove_from_list`	Removes this item from the list:
	`slideshow.slides[3].remove_from_list`

Trees

Let's think about the most complex relationship in Photo Share: nested categories. You could implement categories by adding `belongs_to :category` and `has_many :categories` to the `Category` class. The resulting code would be awkward because a category would have an attribute called `category` (for the parent) and another called `categories` for the children. `parent` and `children` attributes would be better, but you'd be forced to override Active Record naming conventions and to write much more code.

This arrangement is common enough that Active Record has the `acts_as_tree` relationship, shown in Figure 4-6. Just as you did with `acts_as_list`, you will need to install a plug-in.

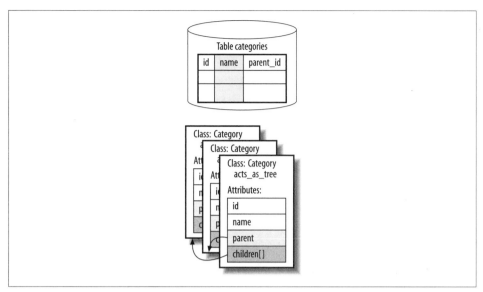

Figure 4-6. The acts_as_tree relationship is recursive, with an entity (Category) acting as both parent and children

```
$ script/plugin install acts_as_tree
+ ./README
+ ./Rakefile
+ ./init.rb
+ ./lib/active_record/acts/tree.rb
...
```

acts_as_tree requires a foreign key called parent_id by default. Recall that we added parent_id to photos as part of the initial photos create_categories migration in Chapter 2. If you choose to use the default foreign key, Active Record will find it. Otherwise, you'd have to use the :foreign_key option. The methods and attributes added through acts_as_tree will use the foreign key to organize your tree, adding parent and children attributes to your class so each instance becomes a node of a tree. The root of the tree has a parent id of nil.

You've already got a Category class and a database table behind it with a parent_id. Let's let Active Record manage the app/models/category.rb class:

```
class Category < ActiveRecord::Base
  has_and_belongs_to_many :photos
  acts_as_tree
end
```

If you'd like, you can order the children with :order modifier, but you don't have to. The tree is ready to use as is. You just need a little test data. If you open up *test/fixtures/categories.yml*, you will notice this data is ready to be used:

```
category_1:
  id: 1
```

```
        parent_id: nil
        name: All
      category_2:
        id: 2
        parent_id: 1
        name: People
      category_3:
        id: 3
        parent_id: 1
        name: Animals
      category_4:
        id: 4
        parent_id: 1
        name: Places
      category_5:
        id: 5
        parent_id: 1
        name: Things
      category_6:
        id: 6
        parent_id: 2
        name: Friends
      category_7:
        id: 7
        parent_id: 2
        name: Family
```

The `parent_id` defines the structure of the tree. Notice that the node named `people` has `Friends` and `Family` as children. Also, you can see that the `root` node, called `All`, has nil for a `parent_id`. Start or reload the console:

```
>> root = Category.find_by_parent_id(nil)
=> #<Category id: 1, parent_id: nil, name: "All",
created_at: "2008-05-11 02:27:21", updated_at: "2008-05-11 02:27:21">
>> root.children.collect {|child| child.name}.join(', ')
=> "People, Animals, Things"
>> root.children[0].children.collect {|child| child.name}.join(', ')
=> "Friends, Family"
>> Category.find_by_name('Family').parent.name
=> "People"
```

The children are dependent objects of the parents, so if you delete a parent, you'll delete the children, too. Otherwise, what you've created is identical to a **has_many** relationship and a **belongs_to** relationship on **category**. Table 4-4 shows the methods and attributes added by the **acts_as_tree** relationship.

Table 4-4. Metaprogramming for acts_as_tree

Added feature	Description
Methods	
All methods from has_many	A tree will have all of the methods of a has_many relationship, with children as the <associations> collection:
	`category.children.create`

Added feature	Description
Attributes	
Parent	`category.parent`
Children[]	An array of children:
	`category.children`

What You Haven't Seen

This implementation of categories is like a filesystem. Each directory has a set of files, just as each of our categories has a set of photos. Another macro, called `acts_as_nested_set`, would be useful if you wanted to find all of the folders in the `All` tree. Active Record is too big to cover in detail in such a short book, but we'll point you to a few things that you should know:

Event callbacks
Active Record can call a method when an event happens, such as before a save, after creation, or when a model changes.

Reflection
Active Record will let you find attributes (as you've seen), and will also find all of the associations, or relationships, defined on a model.

Versioning
Active Record uses the column `lock_version`, if it exists, to manage concurrency using a technique called *optimistic locking*. With this technique, a database engine can store multiple versions of each piece of data and maintain database integrity if many applications need the same piece of data.

Count caching
Rather than using SQL to compute the number of certain types of objects, Active Record can cache the number of items in a collection for performance.

Polymorphic associations
You can design a model that has `belongs_to` relationships to more than one model. For example, an `address` can belong to a `person` and a `shipment`.

Enhancements
Active Record gets enhanced often. We recommend that you periodically check the documentation and watch the various Rails mailing lists if you're going to be doing regular Rails development. Most importantly, Rails 2.1 supports dirty tracking and partial updates. You can use new features before they ship in the pre-release version of Rails called Edge Rails.

Looking Ahead

In the first four chapters, you learned how to build models, views, and controllers. In the next few chapters, we'll continue to flesh out the Photo Share application. First, we'll use scaffolding to rapidly build the user interface. Then, we'll extend the resulting application through controllers and views. You'll have a full working application a few hours from now.

## CHAPTER 5

Working with Views

So far, you've taken a quick pass through Rails controllers and views in Chapter 1, where you learned how a basic Rails request works. Then, you took a deeper dive into controllers by using the scaffolding feature to build basic models, views, and controllers for your application in Chapter 2. In Chapters 3 and 4, you fleshed out the Active Record models, adding the relationships you need to make each one of them work for Photo Share.

It may not seem like it, but the lion's share of this demo application is built. Most of the remaining work is related to views and testing. In this chapter, you will learn how to:

- Take control of the views rendered through scaffolding
- Handle relationships in our views through building in links
- Render common pieces of a website (such as a navigation bar) through layouts
- Work with Rails routes to build friendlier URLs
- Reuse shared common pieces of a web page in fragments called *partials*
- Manage CSS styles to keep your application more consistent

The Big Picture

Let's step back for a moment to review the basic processing steps that happen from the time the server receives a URL request to when Rails finally returns the resulting HTML response (affectionately known as *the big picture*):

1. The web server receives a request consisting mostly of a URL, some optional parameters, and a message body. The web server sends the request to the Rails application for handling.

2. The web server will handle requests for static resources, such as images and stylesheets, directly.

3. If the URL does not match a static pattern, the web server forwards the request to Rails.

4. For some configurations, the web server will forward all Rails requests to an intermediate Ruby application server such as Mongrel. For others, a single web server handles all requests.

5. Regardless of the mechanism that the web server uses to forward the request, Rails will handle the request in exactly the same way.

6. Rails forwards requests to the router. The router will get each request to the right piece of the application for processing.

7. The router parses the URL into a hash called `params` based on routing rules in *config/routes.rb* (see Chapter 2 for more details). The router forwards the request to the controller and action defined in the hash.

8. The action accesses any backend systems such as databases or web services. The action then renders a view or redirects the response to another URL. If the action doesn't explicitly render a view or redirect, Rails picks a default view to render.

9. Rails renders a view template to create the HTML response text that is sent back to the browser. The view will have HTML and also mixed in Ruby. Rails uses *ERb* (Embedded Ruby) to execute the Ruby code and place dynamic content into the view.

10. The view template can also render other small templates, called *partials*, and insert them into the view template's output. This approach is great for rendering elements that are used on more than one page or multiple times on a single page because the code won't have to be duplicated.

11. For most sites, Rails will render a layout template along with the primary view. This layout will handle pieces of the web page that are common across the site, such as navigation bars, headers, sidebars, or footers.

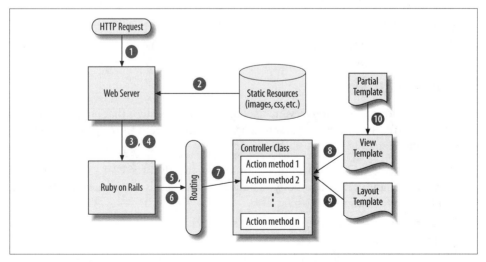

Figure 5-1. Handling an HTTP request

Figure 5-1 shows how it all fits together. This chapter touches briefly on routing, but focuses on steps 8 through 10. In Chapter 6, we'll introduce Ajax, a richer model for building web-based user interfaces. The Ajax model will change this flow, but not by much. First, let's work on those features of Photo Share that need attention.

Seeing Real Photos

This chapter is highly dependent on previous chapters, so if you are implementing this Photo Share application as you read, make sure that you are starting this chapter with the same source code that we have. For example, in the previous chapter, when you generated the scaffolding for each of the database tables, you could easily have let the scaffold generator overwrite the model classes in which we had specified the relationships between the tables.

The easiest way to make sure you are starting with the right code is to download our ZIP file that contains everything we have done up to this point. You can find this file on the book's website: *http://www.oreilly.com/catalog/9780596522001*. You will want to copy over the *config/database.yml.example* file to *config/database.yml* and then update the configuration specifically for your local database.

You also need some real photos to display. That same ZIP file contains sample photos in the *public/images/photos* directory. Of course, you'd normally want the user to upload their own photos, but we'll skip that problem for now so we can focus on building views.

And, finally, make sure that your database contains the same data as ours. Use `rake photos:reset` to recreate the tables and data in your Photo Share database.

View Templates

Photo Share is supposed to be a web application for storing photos, but so far, the scaffolding shows only boring filenames. To make that change, we'll work with view templates and controllers. Edit the file *app/views/photos/show.html.erb*, which is the view template created by the scaffold generator. If you have used template languages like ASP or JSP[*] before, you will recognize the syntax for embedding executable code within the HTML template. In this case, Rails is using ERb to embed Ruby code within an HTML template. As you recall, ERb will execute Ruby code between <% and %> without displaying anything. ERb will execute expressions between <%= and %> and place the results from executing that code into the template.

Insert this line at the beginning of *app/views/photos/show.html.erb*:

```
<%= image_tag 'photos/' + @photo.filename %>
```

[*] ASP is Microsoft's Active Server Pages, and JSP is Sun's Java Server Pages: both are HTML template systems.

This line calls the Rails helper function `image_tag`, which generates an HTML `<img>` tag for the photo's filename. By default, images are expected to be in the *public/images* directory of our Rails app. The photos on PhotoShare are in the *public/images/photos* directory, so prefix the filename with *photos/*. `@photo`, which we set in *app/controllers/photos_controller.rb*, contains the database record for the photos that we want to display:

```
def index
  @photos = Photo.find(:all)

  respond_to do |format|
    format.html # index.html.erb
    format.xml  { render :xml => @photos }
  end
end

def show
  @photo = Photo.find(params[:id])

  respond_to do |format|
    format.html # show.html.erb
    format.xml  { render :xml => @photo }
  end
end
```

Let's see how this looks. Make sure that the web server is started with `script/server`, browse to *http://127.0.0.1:3000/photos*, and click on the Show link for any of the pictures. Now that is much nicer—an actual picture (see Figure 5-2).

Now that you can see the images, it's time to go back and beautify the *photo/index* page. Include the thumbnail image in place of the filename, and make it a clickable link to the *show* page. This strategy lets you eliminate almost everything else about the photo and enables the user go to the show page to see the details. Edit *app/views/photos/index.html.erb* to look like this:

```
<h1>Listing photos</h1>

<table>
  <% for photo in @photos %>
    <tr>
      <td><%= link_to(image_tag("photos/#{photo.thumbnail}",
                                :size => "75x56",
                                :border => 1), photo) %></td>
      <td><%=h photo.filename %></td>
      <td><%= link_to 'delete me', photo, :confirm => 'Are you sure?',
                                    :method => :delete %></td>
    </tr>
  <% end %>
</table>

<br />

<%= link_to 'New photo', new_photo_path %>
```

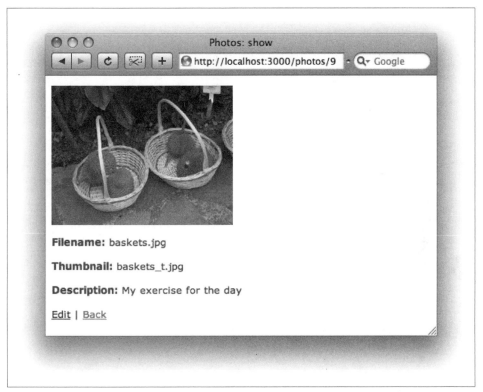

Figure 5-2. Showing an actual photo

There is a lot going on in this code, so we will go through it in considerable detail. First, let's just see how it looks. Browse to *http://127.0.0.1:3000/photos*; you should see something like Figure 5-3. This is starting to look halfway decent.

Let's examine that code in detail:

`<% for photo in @photos %>`
> Rails executes the code between `<%` and `%>`, looping through each database row contained in `@photos`, which contains a list of `Photo` objects set by the controller. Each `Photo`, in turn, is assigned to `photo`.

`"photos/#{photo.thumbnail}"`
> Ruby allows single quotes and double quotes to delimit strings. Ruby evaluates the contents of strings with double quotes, but not single quotes. That evaluation pass will process substitutions. In this example, Ruby substitutes the result of `photo.thumbnail`, at execution time, for `#{photo.thumbnail}`, so this expression is exactly the same as `'photos/' + photo.thumbnail`.

Figure 5-3. Thumbnails in the photo list

```
<%= link_to(image_tag(...), photo) %>
```
The link_to helper function creates a hyperlink. The first parameter is link text or the image to display, and the second parameter is the target URL for the link. Rails will automatically generate the URL for a resource when the Active Record object is given in the parameter.[*]

```
image_tag("photos/#{photo.thumbnail}", :size => '75x56', :border => 1)
```
The image_tag helper function creates an image tag. The first parameter is the path to the thumbnail, and those remaining specify attributes for the image tag.

```
<%=h photo.filename %>
```
The h method creates properly escaped HTML text, so characters like < become <.[†] This line displays the photo's filename, making sure that any special characters are properly escaped. We could have used <%= h(photo.filename) %>, but

---

[*] In Ruby, these parentheses are optional as long as the resulting code is not ambiguous. We include parentheses in this case because the parameters to link_to are themselves method calls.

[†] When you include user-entered text from the database, you want escaped text because you don't know what characters it could contain. A user could accidentally or maliciously enter text that's interpreted as HTML.

this style is more common because it makes the h call look more like it's part of the tag.

```
<%= link_to 'delete me', photo, :confirm => 'Are you sure?',
:method => :delete %>
```

Here, the link_to method is used again. This time, it creates a link to the destroy method of the current controller, but with a couple of twists. First, we use an HTTP DELETE action to satisfy the routing rules covered in Chapter 2. That's why you see the :method => :delete code. Next, we use the :confirm option, which creates a JavaScript pop-up dialog in the browser asking "Are you sure?" If the user answers "OK," the browser follows the link, destroying the photo. If the user cancels, then nothing further happens.

```
<%= link_to 'New photo', new_photo_path %>
```

This code creates a link to new_photo_path. This path, created by the resource :photos statement in *config/routes.rb*, is a shorthand way to specify the new photo form at the URL :controller => 'photos', :action => 'new'. You will see a few more of these paths as we go on.

Layouts

You may have noticed that the HTML pages that we created are incomplete. Rails uses a feature called *layouts* to let you specify a common set of display elements for every page rendered by a controller. This feature is typically useful for common headers, footers, and sidebars. By default, Rails looks in its *app/view/layouts* directory for an *html.erb* file whose name matches the controller's name. Failing that, Rails will look for a file called *application.html.erb*.

Take a look at *app/views/layouts/photos.html.erb*. You should see something like this:

```
<!DOCTYPE html PUBLIC "-//W3C//DTD XHTML 1.0 Transitional//EN"
        "http://www.w3.org/TR/xhtml1/DTD/xhtml1-transitional.dtd">

<html xmlns="http://www.w3.org/1999/xhtml" xml:lang="en" lang="en">
<head>
  <meta http-equiv="content-type" content="text/html;charset=UTF-8" />
  <title>Photos: <%= controller.action_name %></title>
  <%= stylesheet_link_tag 'scaffold' %>
</head>
<body>

<p style="color: green"><%= flash[:notice] %></p>

<%= yield  %>

</body>
</html>
```

This is the layout template for the photos controller. The HTML output created by any action in the photos controller is inserted into the layout where you see the line:

```
<%= yield %>
```

and sent back to the browser for display. `yield` is actually a Ruby command that executes a current code block. The Rails framework passes some code that renders the view to the code that then renders the layout. After that, when you say `yield`, your code neatly executes the code block, dropping the contents of your view into the layout. The end result is a valid HTML page.

Let's create a layout for the entire Photo Share application. By default, Rails looks for a layout file with the same name as the controller, but we don't want Rails to find the simple layouts created by the resource generator. Delete all of the layout files in *app/views/layout*. Next, create an application-wide layout and add some common links that will show at the top of every page. Make the *app/views/layouts/application.html.erb* file look like this:

```
<!DOCTYPE html PUBLIC "-//W3C//DTD XHTML 1.0 Transitional//EN"
        "http://www.w3.org/TR/xhtml1/DTD/xhtml1-transitional.dtd">

<html xmlns="http://www.w3.org/1999/xhtml" xml:lang="en" lang="en">
<head>
  <meta http-equiv="content-type" content="text/html;charset=UTF-8" />
  <title>Photos: <%= controller.action_name %></title>
  <%= stylesheet_link_tag 'scaffold' %>
</head>
<body>

<div style="background-color:LightBlue">
    <p>
       
      <%= link_to 'Photos', photos_path %>
       
      <%= link_to 'Categories', categories_path %>
       
      <%= link_to 'Slideshows', slideshows_path %>
    </p>
</div>

<p style="color: green"><%= flash[:notice] %></p>

<%= yield %>

</body>
</html>
```

As you expected, this text is pure HTML, with a few simple Ruby expressions to link to the `index` actions for photos, categories, and slideshows. The contents of individual views will appear in place of the yield. Now, you can click on any link, and every page in this Photo Share application will have this navigation bar at the top.

Setting the Default Root

Typing *http://127.0.0.1:3000/photos* or *http://localhost:3000/photos* is getting tedious. It would be easier to use *http://127.0.0.1:3000/* and be directed to whatever page you want to designate as the starting page. You already know how Rails specifies routes. Edit *config/routes.rb* and find this section of comments:

```
# You can have the root of your site routed with map.root --
# just remember to delete public/index.html.
# map.root :controller => "welcome"
```

Now, uncomment the last line and change it to:

```
map.root :controller => "photos"
```

With this new routing rule, anytime Rails sees an empty URL (represented by the '' parameter), it will invoke the `index` action in the `photos` controller. Before this change will work, you need to delete the *public/index.html* file. If you don't, the web server will serve up *public/index.html* instead of *app/views/photos/index.html.erb* whenever you browse to *http://127.0.0.1:3000/*. Because the *index.html* is static, Rails will never get called.

Now, try browsing to *http://127.0.0.1:3000/*; you should see a nice new *photos/index* page, complete with thumbnails and navigation bar.

Stylesheets

Currently, to change the styling of the application, you have to change each individual HTML element. If you've used much HTML, you know that our current design will make design work tedious and error prone. Before we get too far along in beautifying our Photo Share application, we should start using stylesheets to keep all styling in one place. First, we'll create an overall application stylesheet where we will move the styles for our navigation bar and set a background color for all pages. Then, we'll create a special stylesheet for specifying styles for our photos and thumbnails.

Rails creates a *public/stylesheets/scaffold.css* file that contains the basic styling used by generated scaffolding code. Let's use this as a starting point for our application's overall stylesheet. Copy the file *public/stylesheets/scaffold.css* and name this copy *public/stylesheets/application.css*.

First, change the background color to a very light gray by adding `background: #eee;` to the section starting `body, p, ol, ul, td {`. Then, add a `.navbar` section to style the navigation bar. When you're done, the beginning of *application.css* should look like this:

```
body { background-color: #fff; color: #333; }

body, p, ol, ul, td {
  font-family: verdana, arial, helvetica, sans-serif;
```

```
    font-size:    13px;
    line-height: 18px;
       background: #eee;
}

.navbar {
    padding: 7px;
    padding-bottom: 12px;
    margin-bottom: 20px;
    background-color: LightBlue;
}

pre {
...
```

Next, edit the standard layout file (*app/views/layouts/application.html.erb*) and replace the styling information for the navigation bar with a reference to the stylesheet. Edit *app/views/layouts/application.html.erb* to look like this:

```
<!DOCTYPE html PUBLIC "-//W3C//DTD XHTML 1.0 Transitional//EN"
      "http://www.w3.org/TR/xhtml1/DTD/xhtml1-transitional.dtd">

<html xmlns="http://www.w3.org/1999/xhtml" xml:lang="en" lang="en">
<head>
  <meta http-equiv="content-type" content="text/html;charset=UTF-8" />
  <title>Photos: <%= controller.action_name %></title>
  <%= stylesheet_link_tag 'application' %>
</head>
<body>

<div style="background-color:LightBlue">
    <p class="navbar">
       
      <%= link_to 'Photos', photos_path %>
       
      <%= link_to 'Categories', categories_path %>
       
      <%= link_to 'Slideshows', slideshows_path %>
    </p>
</div>

<p style="color: green"><%= flash[:notice] %></p>

<%= yield  %>

</body>
</html>
```

stylesheet_link_tag creates a link to the *application.css* file; adding class="navbar" to the paragraph tag displays it with our .navbar styles.

Let's see how this looks. If you browse to *http://127.0.0.1:3000/*, it should look like Figure 5-4.

Figure 5-4. Using a stylesheet

Now, let's style the photo thumbnails to have a visual frame. Create the file *public/stylesheets/photos.css* containing this:

```
#thumbnail {
    padding: 1em;
    background: #ddd;
    border: thin solid #333;
}
```

Edit *app/views/layouts/application.html.erb* and change `stylesheet_link_tag` to `<%= stylesheet_link_tag 'application', 'photos' %>`. Then, edit *app/views/photos/index.html.erb* and add an `:id => 'thumbnail'` attribute to the image tag. That part of *index.html.erb* should look like this:

```
<%= link_to(image_tag("photos/#{photo.thumbnail}",
                :size => '75x56',
                :border => 1,
                :id => 'thumbnail'),
        photo
    )
%>
```

Browse to *http://127.0.0.1:3000/*. It should look like Figure 5-5.

Figure 5-5. Using a stylesheet to display borders on the pictures

Things are starting to look pretty good.* Now we need to assign photos to categories. Also, we must be able to create and edit categories.

Hierarchical Categories

When we generated scaffold code for categories, we got some basic CRUD screens. But they ignore the fact that our categories are hierarchical. The basic problem is every category item has a parent (except for the root category), and there is no way in the CRUD screens to specify the parent of a category.

For now, we are going to fix this in a very simple way that will get you get up and running quickly. There will be plenty of time later for a fancier user interface.

Every category has a name, but these names are not always individually unique because they are qualified by their parents in the hierarchy. For example, you might have two

---

* The borders will look a little different in Microsoft's Internet Explorer (as opposed to Firefox, shown here), due to differences in CSS handling.

categories named *Car*, but one of them might have a parent named *Bruce* while the other has a parent named *Curt*. A unique identifier for a category would prefix the category name with all of its parents. So, for these two *Car* categories, we might have long names like *All:Bruce:Car* and *All:Curt:Car*. Let's implement this attribute as a long_name attribute in our Category model. Edit *app/models/category.rb* to look like this:

```
class Category < ActiveRecord::Base
  has_and_belongs_to_many :photos
  acts_as_tree
  def ancestors_name
    if parent
      parent.ancestors_name + parent.name + ':'
    else
      ""
    end
  end

  def long_name
    ancestors_name + name
  end
end
```

The long_name method returns a string that is the concatenation of the names of all of its parents with its own name. ancestors_name is a recursive method that concatenates all of the parent names with a ":" separator. You can see this working on our category index page. Edit the categories controller, *app/controllers/categories_controller.rb*, and change the index action to this:

```
def index
  @all_categories = Category.find(:all, :order=>"name")
end
```

Now, edit the corresponding view template, *app/views/categories/index.html.erb*, to look like this:

```
<h1>Listing categories</h1>

<table>
  <tr>
    <th>Name</th>
  </tr>

<% for category in @all_categories %>
  <tr>
    <td><%=h category.long_name %></td>
    <td><%= link_to 'Edit', edit_category_path(category) %></td>
    <td><%= link_to 'Destroy', :confirm => 'Are you sure?', :method => :delete %></td>
  </tr>
<% end %>
</table>

<br />

<%= link_to 'New category', new_category_path %>
```

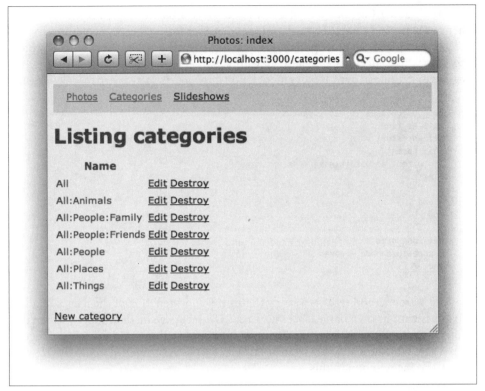

Figure 5-6. Showing category hierarchy

The new code is in bold, and the code dealing with pagination and displaying multiple columns has been removed; plus, the *show* link was removed because the show page doesn't display anything you can't already see on the list page.

The second bolded line calls the new `long_name` method.

Figure 5-6 shows what you'll see when you browse to *http://127.0.0.1:3000/categories*.

When you look at the forms for editing and creating a category, you'll see that they are the same. We can save ourselves from a little duplication by breaking out the form piece of these templates into a piece of shared code called a *partial*. Edit *app/views/categories/edit.html.erb*, making it render a partial, like this:

```
<h1>Editing category</h1>

<% form_for(@category) do |f| %>
<%= render :partial => 'form', :locals => { :f => f } %>
  <p>
    <%= f.submit "Update" %>
  </p>
<% end %>
```

```
<%= link_to 'Show', @category %> |
<%= link_to 'Back', categories_path %>
```

Do the same thing for *app/views/categories/new.html.erb*:

```
<h1>New category</h1>

<% form_for(@category) do |f| %>
<%= render :partial => 'form', :locals => { :f => f } %>
  <p>
    <%= f.submit "Create" %>
  </p>
<% end %>

<%= link_to 'Back', categories_path %>
```

Now, you can have one file instead of two that renders the form fields that you saw in new and edit. Create a new file called *app/views/categories/_form.html.erb*. Don't miss the underscore, which identifies the file as a partial:

```
<%= f.error_messages %>

<p>
    <%= f.label :name %><br />
    <%= f.text_field :name %>
</p>
```

Next, modify the new and edit views to let you pick the category's parent. Fortunately, both views now use the common *app/views/categories/_form.html.erb* to display a category form, so that's the only view template you need to modify:

```
<%= f.error_messages %>

<p>
    <%= f.label :name %><br />
    <%= f.text_field :name %>
</p>
<p>
    <%= f.label :parent_id %><br />
    <%= f.collection_select :parent_id, @all_categories, :id, :long_name %>
</p>
```

This code uses the form helper collection_select, which generates HTML <select> and <option> tags to create a drop-down select list.

The first parameters to collection_select specify the attribute on the category that this control will set. (The form tag in the new and edit views both specify a category.) The remaining three parameters specify the list of choices the user will have. @all_categories is a list of objects containing the valid choices. :id and :long_name specify the object attributes that get the key value and display value for each choice. For example, the categories list will show all of the long_name values of all of the categories in the @all_categories array. When the user picks a category, Rails will post a hash called category that will set the parent_id attribute to the id of the category that the user picked.

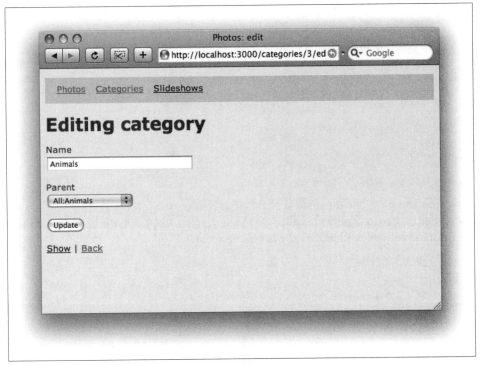

Figure 5-7. Drop-down category selection

For this new form to work, you need to set `@all_categories` in the controller for the edit and new methods:

```
def new
  @category = Category.new
  @all_categories = Category.find(:all, :order=>"name")
end

...

def edit
  @category = Category.find(params[:id])
  @all_categories = Category.find(:all, :order=>"name")
end
```

Click the Edit link for any category to see the results of your handiwork (as shown in Figure 5-7).

Assign a Category to a Photo

Let's update our photo CRUD pages so you can assign categories to a `photo`. For now, we will take a simple approach like we did with categories.

As with categories, the edit photo and new photo pages will use a common partial view template named _form.html.erb. As mentioned earlier, a *partial* is a small template that does not render an entire page, but just a small, reusable element. This is great for rendering elements that are used on more than one page because the code won't have to be duplicated. Create a new file called *app/views/photos/_form.html.erb* to present all of the input fields that the form will need:

```
<%= f.error_messages %>

<p>
    <%= f.label :filename %><br />
  <%= f.text_field :filename %>
</p>
<p>
    <%= f.label :thumbnail %><br />
  <%= f.text_field :thumbnail %>
</p>
<p>
    <%= f.label :description %><br />
  <%= f.text_field :description %>
</p>
<p>
    <%= f.label :categories %><br />
  <%= f.collection_select :category_ids, @all_categories, :id, :long_name, {},
      { :multiple => true } %>
</p>
```

We'll need to use the partial in two actions: create and edit. First, edit *app/views/photos/ edit.html.erb* to render the partial, passing in the form variable:

```
<h1>Editing photo</h1>

<% form_for(@photo) do |f| %>
<%= render :partial => 'form', :locals => { :f => f } %>
  <p>
    <%= f.submit "Update" %>
  </p>
<% end %>

<%= link_to 'Show', @photo %> |
<%= link_to 'Back', photos_path %>
```

Now, edit *app/views/photos/new.html.erb* in the same way:

```
<h1>New photo</h1>

<% form_for(@photo) do |f| %>
<%= render :partial => 'form', :locals => { :f => f } %>
  <p>
    <%= f.submit "Create" %>
  </p>
<% end %>

<%= link_to 'Back', photos_path %>
```

This code slightly refactors the scaffold to use a single form in two different places to reduce repetition. The `collection_select` control creates a multiple-selection HTML listbox populated with the category objects in the instance variable `@all_categories` using the `id` of each category as the select option's value and the `long_name` of each category as the select option's display text.

Next, you need to add code to the photos controller to set `@all_categories` and then grab the form results that are posted back to update the database. Edit *app/controllers/photos_controller.rb*, and change the `new` and `edit` methods to look like this:

```
def new
  @photo = Photo.new
  @all_categories = Category.find(:all, :order => "name")
    ...
end

def edit
  @photo = Photo.find(params[:id])
  @all_categories = Category.find(:all, :order => "name")
end
```

This is how we're processing categories within the `edit` action. First, the `edit` method retrieves the photo object that has the target `id` and then gets a list of all categories, ordered by name. Next, we make a list of `@all_categories` to populate the multiple selection list. Now, shift your attention to the view. The key line of code is the collection select:

```
<%= f.collection_select :category_ids, @all_categories, :id, :long_name, {},
  { :multiple => true } %>
```

The collection select control in the view has a bit of dark magic, so we'll walk through it in more depth this time around. Notice that `collection_select` is a method on `f`. Recall that `f` is a form for a `photo`. Next is the name of the attribute. The suffix on `category_ids` tells Rails to check an external association called `categories`. For the inbound form, Rails will build a control with the appropriate categories preselected. For the outbound form data upon submit, Rails will create a list of category ids with this name. Based on this field name, Rails knows to use `@photo.categories` to get a list of category objects, one for each category assigned to the photo.

After defining the object and attribute, we define the list of all categories and provide some metadata that Rails can use to interpret the list. The `@all_categories` variable that we set in the controller will populate the selection list. The two important attributes to items on that list are the key/value pair of `:id` and `:long_name`. Rails will pass key/value pairs back to the controller for every selected object in the list.

So, when the user submits the form, Rails creates a hash for `photo`, including a list of selected category ids, and delivers it to the controller. When the controller calls `@photo.update_attributes` with the photo hash, Active Record updates all of the properties on `Photo`, including all of the associated categories. Very nice!

That's all there is to it. You can now assign multiple categories to each photo. Give it a try! You should be starting to see how easy it is to incrementally build out your Photo Share application. There's no special deploy step, and you don't have to reboot the server for each change, unless you make a major change like installing a new plug-in or renaming your database.

Styling the Slideshows

Now that you've implemented a complex relationship, it's time to spice things up a bit. Let's take stock of where we are with the Photo Share application:

- We have created a common layout that displays navigation links on every page to the three major areas: photos, categories, and slideshows.
- The pages that deal with photos look pretty good.
- The pages that deal with categories are functional, but could use some improvement.
- We're using cascading stylesheets to specify the visual styling of our pages and their elements.

We haven't yet done anything with the slideshows, which are still using the generated scaffolding. The page that displays a list of all slideshows is the focal point that links to all the things you can do with slideshows: create them, edit them, delete them, and play them. Fixing up this page will have a tremendous visual impact, so this is a good place to start.

Currently, the list slideshows page looks like Figure 5-8. This is definitely ugly!

In the process of getting to this goal, you will learn about many new features. At the moment, we've defined only one slideshow, but later on you will create more slideshows.

The slideshow controller's list action already gets the needed information from the database, so you don't need to modify *app/controllers/slideshows_controller.rb*. The index method looks like this:

```
def index
  @slideshows = Slideshow.find(:all)
    ...
end
```

You'll want to use the `@slideshows` instance variable in your view template because it contains a list of `Slideshow` objects to display. You've seen this code before; it is used (in this case) to break up long lists of slideshows into bite-size chunks.

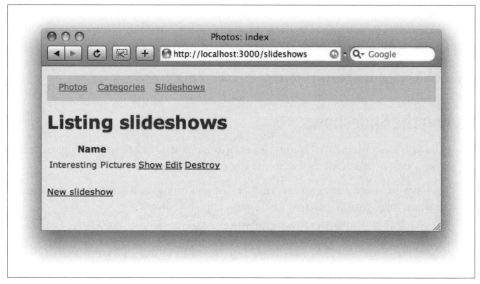

Figure 5-8. Current (ugly) slideshow listing

Edit the view template (*app/views/slideshows/index.html.erb*) to make it look like this:

```
<p><%= link_to 'New slideshow', new_slideshow_path %></p>

<div id="slideshow-summaries">
<% for slideshow in @slideshows %>
  <div class="slideshow-summary">
    <div class="slideshow-caption">
        <%= slideshow.name %>
        <small>(<%= slideshow.slides.size %> slides)</small>
    </div>

    <div class="slideshow-thumbnails">
        <% 5.times do |i| -%>
            <%= thumbnail_tag slideshow.slides[i] %>
        <% end -%>
         <strong>. . .</strong>
    </div>

    <div class="slideshow-controls">
        <%= link_to 'Play', slideshow %>
        <%= link_to 'Edit', edit_slideshow_path(slideshow) %>
        <%= link_to 'Delete', slideshow, :confirm => 'Are you sure?',
    :method => :delete %>
        </div>
  </div>
  <br />
<% end %>
</div>

<br />
```

This first thing you should notice is that we are using nested `<div>` tags instead of tables to format the contents. Using `<div>` tags gives you a lot more flexibility and power when specifying the styling options in the CSS stylesheet. Each display element is contained within its own `<div>` section with a unique `id` attribute. You'll use these same `div` names in the stylesheet to determine how each element is displayed. We'll create the stylesheet shortly, but first, let's go through the code in this template:

```
<% for slideshow in @slideshows %>
```

You saw this line before in the photos list template. It loops through each database row contained in `@slideshows` (which was set by the controller), assigning each, in turn, to `slideshow`.

```
<div class="slideshow-caption">
    <%= slideshow.name %>
    <small>(<%= slideshow.slides.size %> slides)</small>
</div>
```

This `div` is simply a caption block that displays the name of the slideshow along with the number of photos it contains.

```
<div class="slideshow-thumbnails">
    <% 5.times do |i| -%>
        <%= thumbnail_tag slideshow.slides[i] %>
    <% end -%>
     <strong>. . .</strong>
</div>
```

This `div` shows a little preview of the slideshow by displaying the thumbnails of the first five photos in the slideshow.

```
<div class="slideshow-controls">
    <small>
        <%= link_to 'Play', slideshow %>
        <%= link_to 'Edit', edit_slideshow_path(slideshow) %>
        <%= link_to 'Delete', slideshow, :confirm => 'Are you sure?',
    :method => :delete %>
    </small>
</div>
```

Once again, this `div` should be self-explanatory. It displays a block of links for operating on this particular slideshow. It includes links to play, edit, and delete the slideshow.

When you try to list slideshows, this code breaks. Rails does not have a helper function to display thumbnails, but we'll remedy that next.

Creating Your Own Helper Functions

Rails has many built-in helper functions to assist in creating the HTML that is sent back to the browser, and we have used many of them in our Photo Share application. You can also create your own helper functions.

You can create two kinds of helper functions. Helper functions that you want to be accessible from any controller or view template are application-level helper functions; they go in the file *app/helpers/application_helper.rb*. Helper functions that are specific to a particular controller go in *app/helpers/ <controller-name> _helper.rb*.

We need to implement the `thumbnail_tag` helper that we used earlier. Because it's specific to the `slideshows_controller`, we'll add it to *app/helpers/slideshows_helper.rb*. All views rendered by the `slideshows_controller` will be able to use this helper. Edit *app/helpers/slideshows_helper.rb*, and add the following code inside the module definition:

```
def thumbnail_tag(slide)
  image_tag "photos/#{slide.photo.thumbnail}" if slide
end
```

The meat of the method calls the built-in helper function `image_tag`, passing the path to the slide's thumbnail, thus creating the proper image tag. You may have noticed the view code assumes that there are at least five slides in a slideshow. Because some slideshows may be shorter, you need to allow for `nil`, so add the `if slide` modifier at the end. Because `nil` evaluates to `false`, execute this line of code only if you're given a slide.

Creating the Stylesheet

Remember that we set up our view template with `id=` attributes: for example, `"slideshow-summary"` and `"slideshow-thumbnails"`. This organization lets you create matching entries in your stylesheet to specify their display attributes.

First, let's see what the slideshows listing page looks like *before* you create the stylesheet. Then, you'll really appreciate how easily a stylesheet can improve the look of your page. Make sure the server is started, and browse to *http://127.0.0.1:3000/slideshows*; you should see something like Figure 5-9.

This page is definitely nicer than the earlier version, but it's not as nice as it could be. Now, let's create the stylesheet. Create the file *public/stylesheets/slideshows.css* with the following contents.

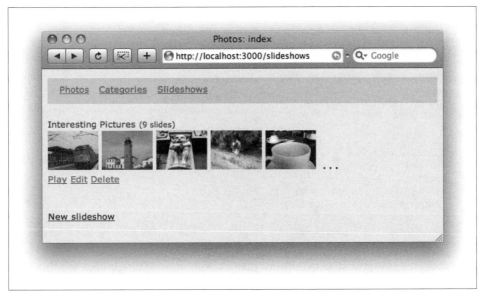

Figure 5-9. Before stylesheet

```
#slideshow-summaries {
    padding: 0.5em;
    float: left;
    background: #ccc;
    margin-left: auto;
    margin-right: auto;
    border-left: thin solid #777;
    border-bottom: thin solid #777;
    border-top: thin solid #aaa;
    border-right: thin solid #aaa;
}

.slideshow-summary {
    padding: 0.5em;
    margin: 0.5em;
    width: 40em;
    float: left;
    background: #ddd;
    border-left: thin solid #777;
    border-bottom: thin solid #777;
    border-top: thin solid #aaa;
    border-right: thin solid #aaa;
}

.slideshow-thumbnails {
    padding: 0.50em;
    background: #eee;
    border-left: thin solid #aaa;
    border-bottom: thin solid #aaa;
    border-top: thin solid #777;
    border-right: thin solid #777;
```

```
}

.slideshow-caption {
   background: #edd;
   border-left: thin solid #aaa;
   border-bottom: thin solid #aaa;
   border-top: thin solid #777;
   border-right: thin solid #777;
   font-size: 1.0em;
}

.slideshow-controls {
   margin-top: 0.50em;
   padding: 0.25em;
   border-left: thin solid #777;
   border-bottom: thin solid #777;
   border-top: thin solid #aaa;
   border-right: thin solid #aaa;
}
```

For the most part, these style definitions just set borders and background shading. For Rails to be able to find the stylesheet, you must include a reference to this stylesheet in your HTML pages. Edit *app/views/layouts/application.html.erb*, and insert:

```
<%= stylesheet_link_tag 'slideshows' %>
```

immediately after the other stylesheet references.

Now, if you refresh your browser, you should see something like Figure 5-10.

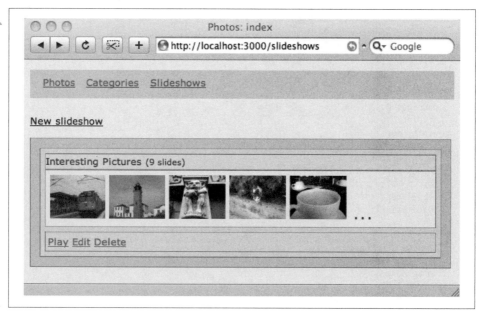

Figure 5-10. After stylesheet

That's much better, although we still need to implement the ability to create, edit, and play a slideshow. We'll tackle that in the next chapter because we're going to use the built-in Ajax facilities in Rails to create an intuitive Ajax user interface.

## CHAPTER 6

Ajax

A few years ago, the Rails support for Ajax was revolutionary. Now, good Ajax support is expected from any web framework. Ajax is a technique for building web pages that are more interactive and dynamic. To use it, you'll use JavaScript libraries to communicate with the server at any time, and the web page need not be frozen while waiting for a response. Rails will simplify Ajax by using helpers to generate JavaScript code, so that in the typical case, you won't use JavaScript at all.

Ajax applications have a few major differences from typical web apps. First, any web page can communicate with the server at any time, and not just by submitting forms and following links. Second, you can update any part of a page at any time. Users get a more responsive site with immediate feedback. Even though using Ajax techniques usually requires significantly more sophisticated design and implementation skills, the benefits to the end user are so great that Ajax-enabled web applications are becoming the rule, not the exception. Fortunately, Rails makes Ajax so simple that, for typical cases, using Ajax is almost as easy as not using it.

How Rails Implements Ajax

Rails has a simple, consistent model for how it implements Ajax operations. Once the browser renders the initial web page, different user actions cause it to display a new web page (like any traditional web application) or trigger an Ajax operation:

Some trigger fires
> This trigger could be the user clicking on a button or link, the user making changes to the data on a form or in a field, or just a periodic trigger (based on a timer).

The web client calls the server
> A JavaScript method, `XMLHttpRequest`, sends data associated with the trigger to an action handler on the server. The data might be the `id` of a checkbox, the text in an entry field, or a whole form.

The server does something
> The server-side action handler—a Rails controller action (for our purposes)—does something with the data and returns an HTML fragment to the web client.

The client receives the response
> The client-side JavaScript, which Rails creates automatically, receives the HTML fragment and uses it to update a specified part of the current page's HTML, often the content of a `<div>` tag.

These steps are the simplest way to use Ajax in a Rails application, but with a little extra work, you can have the server return any kind of data in response to an Ajax request, and you can create custom JavaScript in the browser to perform more involved interactions. We'll stick to HTML fragments in this chapter.

Rails uses the *Prototype* and *script.aculo.us* JavaScript libraries to implement browser support for Ajax. You can use these libraries independently, but with their seamless integration with Rails, you won't need to. Throughout this chapter, we'll exploit the Ajax and special effects capabilities that come with Rails to implement missing features in our Photo Share application.

Playing a Slideshow

Let's see what happens when we try to play a slideshow. Browse to *http://127.0.0.1:3000/slideshows*, and click the Play link for our only slideshow. As you can see in Figure 6-1, this URL invokes the *show* action on the *slideshow* controller, but the action is still using the scaffold code.

We need to change this page to actually "play" the slideshow by sequentially displaying the pictures contained in the slideshow. To do this, we will initially display the first picture in the slideshow. Then, once every two seconds, we'll make an Ajax call to get and display the next picture.

The controller sets up all the slides in a slideshow for playback. You need to start `@slideshow` with the current slideshow set to play. You also need to put the current slide (initially, 0) and the whole slideshow into a holding area called the *session*, so you won't have to read from the database each time you play a new slide. Edit the slideshows controller (*app/controllers/slideshows_controller.rb*), and modify the `show` method to look like this:

```
def show
  @slideshow = Slideshow.find(params[:id])
  session[:slideshow] = @slideshow
  session[:slide_index] = 0
  @slide = @slideshow.slides[0]
end
```

Every two seconds in this code (once we've updated the view code), the browser sends an Ajax request to get the next slide. You can't use instance variables to keep track of where you are in the slideshow because instance variables exist only until you finish processing the current request. Use the Rails-provided session object instead, which is persistent across requests. Let's look at this code in a little more detail.

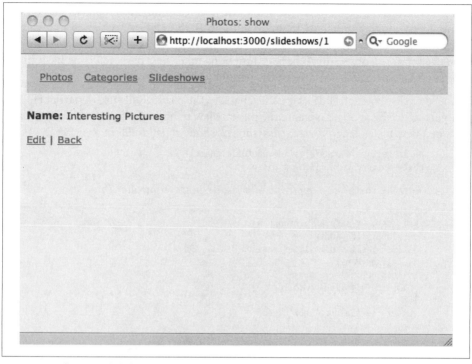

Figure 6-1. Playing a slideshow that still uses scaffolding

`session[:slideshow] = @slideshow` stores a reference to the current slideshow in the session hash at the key `:slideshow` and the index of the currently displayed slide. We initially set the `slide_index` to zero to point to the first slide, and our Ajax request increments the index by one as it displays each slide. We can retrieve these values from the session hash during the Ajax requests for the next slide.

Now, edit the view template (*app/views/slideshows/show.html.erb*) to look like this:

```
<p><i><%=h @slideshow.name %></i></p>

<% if @slide %>
<div id="slides">
    <%= render :partial => "show_slide" %>
</div>

<%= periodically_call_remote :update => "slides",
                             :url => { :action => :show_slide },
                             :frequency => 2.0 %>
<% end %>
```

This ERb template contains three things: a title line, the `div` that displays the current slide, and a magic Ajax incantation that we will now pick apart.

Like all helpers, `periodically_call_remote` generates text. In this case, the text is a JavaScript function that periodically sends a remote Ajax request to our controller. The controller returns an HTML fragment, and the JavaScript function replaces the content of the update target, an HTML element with an `id` of `'slides'`, which is a `<div>` tag. All of this happens without a new page load. The frequency parameter makes the call once every two seconds. All Ajax help functions take their parameters as hash maps with key/value pairs, so you can list the parameters in any order.

We need to display each slide as it comes back to the client; Rails uses a partial HTML template to do this work. To create the partial view template, place the following contents in a new file called *app/views/slideshows/_show_slide.html.erb*:

```erb
<%= image_tag "photos/#{@slide.photo.filename}" %>
<p><%= @slide.photo.filename %></p>
```

and its controller method in *app/controllers/slideshows_controller.rb*:

```ruby
def show_slide
  @slideshow = session[:slideshow]
  session[:slide_index] += 1
  @slide = @slideshow.slides[session[:slide_index]]
  if @slide == nil
    session[:slide_index] = 0
    @slide = @slideshow.slides[0]
  end
  render :partial => "show_slide"
end
```

This method retrieves the slideshow information from the session, moves to the next slide (or back to the beginning if at the end), and then explicitly renders the partial view template `show_slide`. You need to render a partial view or render with the option `:render_layout => false`. Otherwise, Rails tries to render a full template, including layout. As our page already has a layout, simply render a partial template, consisting of an image tag for the slide, and its name.

Finally, you need to update your standard layout template to include script tags for the Prototype JavaScript library because the client-side JavaScript code that Rails creates for you uses them, so in *app/views/layouts/application.html.erb*, insert this line immediately after the title tags:

```erb
<%= javascript_include_tag :defaults %>
```

This line includes three JavaScript files that are shipped with Rails: *prototype.js* and two *Script.aculos.us* files, *effects.js* and *dragdrop.js*. We will use these last two shortly.

Now, show a slideshow by loading *slideshows* and clicking show, and you will see the actual pictures in the slideshow, which change every two seconds.

Using Drag-and-Drop to Reorder Slides

The scaffolding we have for editing a slideshow shows just the slideshow attributes that are stored directly in the *slideshows* table: the slideshow's name and the creation date. The most important part is missing: the photos that are part of the slideshow!

By now, you've probably realized that this is because the scaffolding code deals with only one database table: the *slideshows* table. The relationship data about which photos are assigned to a slideshow and their order in the slideshow are stored in the *slides* table. Let's remedy that problem by adding some Ajax code to deal with slides and the order of the slides.

We're going to display a list of thumbnails of all the photos that are in a slideshow, and then let the user reorder them using drag-and-drop. If you've had to struggle through implementing drag-and-drop before, you're not going to believe how easy this is going to be. Here's a hint: this will take fewer than 50 additional lines of the Ruby, CSS, and ERb template!

Let's start by reviewing the current implementation of the `edit` action in the slideshow controller:

```ruby
def edit
  @slideshow = Slideshow.find(params[:id])
end
```

This action expects to find the `id` of the slideshow to edit passed in as the `id` parameter, which is normally decoded from the URL. You'll find the slideshow with that `id` and assign that slideshow object to the instance variable `@slideshow` so that it can be accessed in the view template.

That is really all that's needed here, so you won't have to add any code to this method. The changes will start with the edit view template, so edit the template *app/views/slideshows/edit.html.erb* and make it look like this:

```erb
<h1>Editing slideshow</h1>

<%= link_to 'Play this slideshow', :action => 'show', :id => @slideshow %>

<div id='slideshow-contents'>
    <%= render :partial => 'show_slides_draggable' %>
</div>

<div id='slideshow-attributes'>
    <% form_for(@slideshow) do |f| %>
      <%= f.error_messages %>

      <p>
        <%= f.label :name %><br />
        <%= f.text_field :name %>
      </p>
      <p>
        <%= f.submit "Update" %>
      </p>
    <% end %>
</div>
```

Notice that we've wrapped the existing `form_for` tag in a `<div>` tag with an `id` attribute of `slideshow-attributes`. You will use this name in one of your CSS files to control the display properties of this section.

There is also a completely new section that displays thumbnails of the photos in the slideshow:

```
<div id='slideshow-contents'>
  <%= render :partial => 'show_slides_draggable' %>
</div>
```

This code also uses a `<div>` tag with an `id` attribute for the same reason: to use a CSS file to control its appearance. This `div` also renders a new partial view template named `show_slides_draggable`, which we will create next.

Create the file *app/views/slideshows/_show_slides_draggable.html.erb* with the following contents:

```
<ol id='sortable_thumbs'>
  <%= render :partial => 'sortable_slide', :collection => @slideshow.slides %>
</ol>

<%= sortable_element('sortable_thumbs',
                  :url => { :action => 'update_slide_order'}) %>
```

Next, create *app/views/slideshows/_sortable_slide.html.erb*, which will have the actual slide:

```
<li id='thumbs_<%= sortable_slide.id %>' class='slides'>
  <%= thumbnail_tag sortable_slide %>
</li>
```

The first part is pretty standard stuff. We're creating an HTML ordered list, in which each list item is a thumbnail image of one of the photos in the slideshow (note that the `thumbnail_tag` helper function was created earlier). The last two lines do the heavy lifting.

`sortable_element` is a helper function that generates the JavaScript code that turns our list into a user-sortable, drag-and-drop-capable list. It wraps this list in an HTML form, and the `:url` option specifies the URL to post to the server whenever the user changes the order of the list. In this case, it calls the action method `update_slide_order` in our slideshow controller. This call works in the background using an Ajax call.

The `update_slide_order` method is pretty simple as well. Edit *app/controllers/slide-shows_controller.rb*, and add this method:

```
def update_slide_order
  params[:sortable_thumbs].each_with_index do |id, position|
    Slide.update(id, :position => position)
  end
end
```

This method iterates through each slide in the list, extracting its id and position in the list, and uses this information to update that slide's database row with its new position. Let's walk through this code in a little more detail:

- params is a hash that holds all the parameters sent to the server in the HTTP request. params[:sortable_thumbs] retrieves the parameter for the sortable_thumbs list, which is an ordered array of the IDs of each thumbnail in the list.
- each_with_index is a Ruby iterator that, just like the each iterator, walks through the array one item at a time. But on each iteration, each_with_index passes to the code block both the object held in the array and its index.
- Slide.update(id, :position => position) then calls the Slide model class to update the slide identified by id with its new position.

We're almost ready to give it a try, but first, let's edit *public/stylesheets/slideshows.css* and add some formatting instructions for the two div IDs we created. Add the following at the end of the file:

```
#slideshow-contents {
    float: left;
    width: 11em;
    padding: 0.50em;
    text-align: center;
    border-right: thin solid #bbb;
    padding: 0.50em;
    padding-bottom: 10em;
}

#slideshow-attributes {
    margin-left: 23em;
    padding-left: 1.5em;
    padding-top: 1.5em;
}
```

This stylesheet displays a list of Slideshow thumbnail images down the left side of the page with the Slideshow attributes immediately to the right of the thumbnails.

Let's see how this looks. Browse to *http://127.0.0.1:3000/slideshows*, and click the edit link for our one and only slideshow. It will look like Figure 6-2.

Click on one of the photos, and try dragging it around. When you drop it into a new location, the JavaScript code on the client triggers the function update_slide_order to write the new order to the database.

Let's fix one minor thing here before we move on. Wouldn't it be better to see the number of each photo appear vertically aligned in the middle of the thumbnail instead of at the bottom? Because our own helper function thumbnail_tag creates the HTML for each thumbnail image, we just need to edit that function and add a vertical-align style attribute.

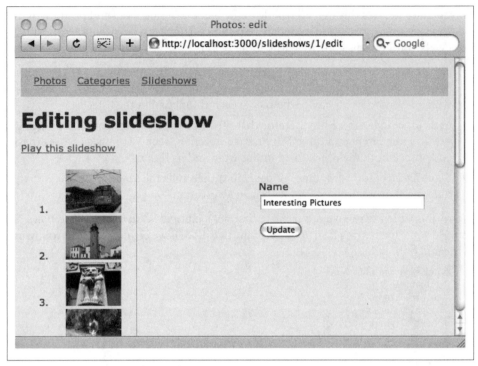

Figure 6-2. A drag-and-drop list of photos

First, edit *app/helpers/slideshows_helper.rb* to look like this:

```
module SlideshowsHelper
  def thumbnail_tag(slide)
    image_tag("photos/#{slide.photo.thumbnail}",
      :style=>"vertical-align:middle"), if slide
      :class => "photos") if slide
    end
end
```

Now, refresh your browser: the list numbers are nicely centered, as you can see in Figure 6-3.

With a very small amount of code, we added a very nice drag-and-drop user interface for reordering the slides in a slideshow. But we're just getting started with our Ajax-enabled user interface.

Drag-and-Drop Everything (Almost Everything)

We have already displayed a list of thumbnails of all photos that are in the slideshow and have enabled the user to drag them around to rearrange their order in the slideshow. Now, let's add a second list of thumbnails, showing all photos that are not being used in the slideshow.

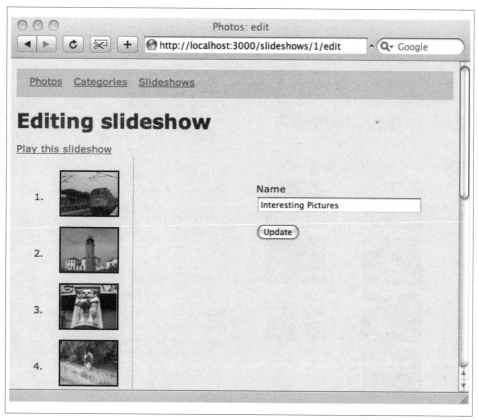

Figure 6-3. Nicely centered list numbers

We'll let the user add a photo to the slideshow by dragging it from the list of unused photos and dropping it onto the slideshow thumbnails. Similarly, we can enable the user to remove a photo from the slideshow by dragging its thumbnail from the slideshow and dropping it on the unused photos list. Finally, we'll allow the user to filter the unused photos list by category.

As you might expect, we can accomplish all of that in a very small amount of code. We will add fewer than 100 lines of code to the models, controllers, view templates, and CSS stylesheet. Figure 6-4 gives you a preview of how this is going to look when we're done.

We're going to work in reverse, starting at the view and working back toward the controller. Let's start by updating the slideshow's edit template. Edit *app/views/slideshows/edit.html.erb* to look like this.

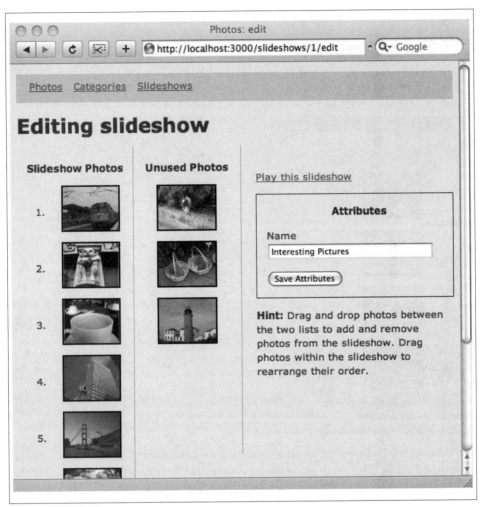

Figure 6-4. Preview of drag-and-drop slideshow editing

```
<h1>Editing slideshow</h1>

<div id='slideshow-contents'>
    <p style='text-align:center;'><b>Slideshow Photos</b></p>
    <div id='showshow-thumbs'>
        <%= render :partial => 'show_slides_draggable' %>
    </div>
</div>

<div id='slideshow-photo-picker'>
    <p style='text-align: center;'><b>Unused Photos</b></p>
    <div id='slideshow-photos'>
        <%= render :partial => 'unused_photo', :collection => @photos %>
    </div>
</div>

<div id='slideshow-attributes'>
    <p><%= link_to 'Play this slideshow', :action => 'show', :id => @slideshow %></p>

    <div style='border: thin solid; padding-left: 1em;'>
        <p style='text-align: center;'><b>Attributes</b></p>
        <% form_for(@slideshow) do |f| %>
            <%= render :partial => 'form', :locals => { :f => f } %>
        <% end %>
    </div>
    <p>
        <b>Hint:</b> Drag and drop photos between the
    two lists to add and remove photos from the
    slideshow. Drag photos within the slideshow to
    rearrange their order.
    </p>
</div>

<%= drop_receiving_element("slideshow-contents", :url => { :action => "add_photo" }) %>
```

This file has been almost entirely rewritten. You can see that we have laid out this edit page into three sections:

```
<div id='slideshow-contents'> ... </div>
<div id='slideshow-photo-picker '> ... </div>
<div id='slideshow-attributes'> ... </div>
```

Only the `slideshow-photo-picker` is new. It shows the list of unused photos that you can add to the slideshow. We will set up the CSS stylesheet to display these sections side-by-side as you saw them in Figure 6-4. The partial template `show_slides_draggable` renders `slideshow-contents`; the partial template `photo_picker` renders `slideshow-photo-picker`; and the `form` partial template mostly renders `slideshow-attributes`. I say "mostly" because I added a few things inline around the rendering of `form`.

Finally, notice two Ajax-related helpers: `drop_receiving_element` and `observe_field`. We'll come back to these in a little bit after we have discussed some prerequisite details.

The last little bit of the view is the edit form in *app/views/slideshows/_form.html.erb*, handling the form elements for each slide:

```
<%= f.error_messages %>

<p>
    <%= f.label :name %><br />
  <%= f.text_field :name %>
</p>
<p>
  <%= f.submit 'Save Attributes' %>
</p>
```

Now, replace the edit method in *app/controllers/slideshows_controller.rb*:

```
def edit
  @slideshow = Slideshow.find(params[:id])
  session[:slideshow] = @slideshow
  @photos = @slideshow.unused_photos
end
```

You next need to create the `unused_photos` method referenced above and the photos method in *app/models/slideshow.rb*:

```
class Slideshow < ActiveRecord::Base
  has_many :slides, :order => 'position'

  def unused_photos
    Photo.find(:all) - photos
  end

  def photos
    slides.map {|slide| slide.photo}
  end
end
```

Let's walk through all of the new code in both the model and view:

`@slideshow = Slideshow.find(params[:id])`
> Here, you retrieve the slideshow for the specified id and store it in the instance variable `@slideshow` to make it available to the view template.

`session[:slideshow] = @slideshow`
> Ajax actions requests will be coming in as the user makes changes, and you need to know what slideshow to change. This line saves a reference to the slideshow in the session hash. I'm using a key value of `:slideshow` to save and retrieve this from the session, but that value is arbitrary and could have been any unique identifier.

`@photos = unused_photos(@slideshow)`
> This line calls the new method `unused_photos` to retrieve a list of all photos that are not in the slideshow; it then saves that list in `@photos`.

```
def unused_photos(slideshow)
```
This method returns a list of photos that are not in the slideshow. The technique used here is inefficient, but it will suffice for now.

We still need to create the *unused_photo* template that generates the HTML to display all the photos that can still be added to a slideshow, so go ahead and create the file *app/views/slideshows/_unused_photo.html.erb* with this in it:

```
<%= image_tag("photos/#{unused_photo.thumbnail}",
      :style => "vertical-align: middle",
      :id => "photo_#{unused_photo.id}",
      :class => "photos") %>
<%= draggable_element "photo_#{unused_photo.id}", :revert => true %>
```

The edit template renders this template for each photo in @photos. For each photo, it uses the image_tag helper to create an HTML image tag and the draggable_element helper to generate the JavaScript code that makes it draggable. You can see that the first parameter of draggable_element matches the value of the id attribute (:id => "photo_#{photo.id}") on the image tag. The draggable_element helper expects the id of the HTML element that it should make draggable, followed by zero or more options. The single option used here (:revert => true) says to move the element back to its original position after it is dropped.

But where can these draggable images be dropped? Recall that at the end of the slideshow's *edit.html.erb* template we had:

```
<%= drop_receiving_element("slideshow-contents",
        :url => {:action => "add_photo" }) %>
```

Just like the draggable_element helper, the drop_receiving_element helper expects the id of the HTML element onto which you can drop something that was declared as draggable. So far, you've done everything needed to handle the inbound Ajax request. It's time to think about what happens in the render part.

When you render a template, you could just decide to render a Rails partial, but let's be a little more elegant. Our template will render a *.rjs* (remote JavaScript) template. These templates define exactly how a controller will use Ajax to update a target web page. Create a file called *views/slideshows/add_photo.rjs* and make it look like this:

```
page.insert_html :bottom, "sortable_thumbs", :partial => 'sortable_slide',
  :locals => { :sortable_slide => @slide }
page.visual_effect :fade, "photo_#{@slide.photo.id}",
  :after_finish => "$('photo_#{@slide.photo.id}').remove"
page.visual_effect :highlight, "sortable_thumbs"
```

This code accomplishes a lot, so let's go through it slowly:

```
page.insert_html :bottom, "sortable_thumbs", :partial => 'sortable_slide', ...
```
This code specifies the first action that will happen when Rails renders this template. The API specifies what to do, where to do it, and which code fragment to

place. It will insert the `sortable_slide` partial at the bottom of the `sortable_thumbs` div.

`page.visual_effect :fade, "photo_#{@slide.photo.id}", :after_finish => ...`

This code specifies the fade visual effect, sliding the `div` with the specified `photo_id` down and removing it when done.

`:highlight, "sortable_thumbs"`

This last code fragment alerts our user to the changes by highlighting `sortable_thumbs`.

Now, we need to create the `add_photo` method to actually add a dropped photo to the slideshow. Edit *app/controllers/slideshows_controller.rb*, adding this method:

```
def add_photo
  photo_id = params[:id].split("_")[1]
  session[:slideshow] = @slideshow = Slideshow.find(session[:slideshow].id)
  @slide = @slideshow.slides.build(:photo_id => photo_id)
  flash[:notice] = 'Error: unable to add photo.' unless @slide.save
end
```

Let's walk through this code:

`slideshow_id = session[:slideshow].id`

This line retrieves the current slideshow from the session hash and gets the slideshow's `id`.

`photo_id = params[:id].split("_")[1]`

The `id` attribute of the dropped photo gets passed as the `:id` parameter. If you recall from the *unused_photo* template, we set those `id`s to values such as `"photo_1"` and `"photo_19"`, so the remainder of this line of code splits the string on the underscore, grabs the second half, and assigns it to `photo_id`.

The next two lines create a new slide, assign to it the photo `id` and the slideshow `id`, and then save it to the database.

Finally, we render the `add_photo.rjs` template.

All of that code handles dragging new photos to add to the slideshow. Now, we just need to add a little more code to implement dragging a photo from the slideshow to the unused photos list as an intuitive way to remove photos from the slideshow.

The displayed photos in the slideshow are already draggable because we made them into a sortable list. The only problem with the current implementation is that the photos can be dragged vertically only. They need to be dragged vertically for reordering *and* horizontally to the unused photos column.

We can only drag the photos vertically because the default option for a sortable list is `:constraint => 'vertical'`. Fortunately, you can change this by editing the file *app/views/slideshows/_show_slides_draggable.html.erb* and changing the call to the `sortable_element` helper to add this `:constraint` option:

```
<%= sortable_element('sortable_thumbs',
                     :url => {:action => 'update_slide_order'},
                     :constraint => '') %>
```

Now you can drag those photos anywhere. But you still need to make the unused photos list into a drop receiver that uses Ajax to remove the dropped photo from the slideshow.

To do so, edit *app/views/slideshows/edit.html.erb,* and add this at the end:

```
<%= drop_receiving_element("slideshow-photo-picker",
           :url => {:action => "remove_slide" }
           ) %>
```

This code is almost identical to the other `drop_receiving_element` we used. The difference is that the target is the `slideshow-photo-picker`, and the action taken on a drop is to call the `remove_slide` method. Also, notice that you can drop only "slides" here (that is, HTML elements with a class attribute of `slides`). If you go back and take a look at how we defined the partial template *app/views/slideshows/_show_slides_draggable.html.erb*, you will see that we did, indeed, make each item in the sortable list a slide.

Add the `remove_slide` method to *app/controllers/slideshows_controller.rb*:

```
def remove_slide
  @slide = Slide.find(params[:id].split("_")[1])
  session[:slideshow] = @slideshow = @slide.slideshow
  @unused_photo = @slide.photo
  @slide.destroy
end
```

Next, create a file called *app/views/slideshows/remove_slides.rjs* with the following contents:

```
page.visual_effect :highlight, "slideshow-photos"
page.insert_html :bottom, "slideshow-photos", :partial => 'unused_photo',
  :locals => { :unused_photo => @unused_photo }
page.visual_effect :SlideUp, "thumbs_#{@slide.id}",
  :after_finish => "$('thumbs_#{@slide.id}').remove"
```

In this code, you get the `id` of slide you want to remove, and then delete it from the slide database table. Remember, this action does not delete the photo from the database. The slide data says what photos are in a given slideshow, and deleting an entry from the slide table removes that slide from its slideshow. Finally, you render the HTML for the photo picker, which now includes the removed slide.

I'll bet you're anxious to see all this in action. All you need to do is to update the stylesheet and then try it out. Edit *public/stylesheets/slideshows.css,* and add the following:

```
#slideshow-photo-picker {
    float: left;
    width: 10em;
    text-align: center;
    border-right: thin solid #bbb;
    padding: 0.5em;
    padding-bottom: 10em;
```

```
}

img.thumbnail {
    border: 2px solid black;
    margin-bottom: 1em;
}

img.photos {
    border: 2px solid black;
    margin-bottom: 1em;
}
```

Whew! That's it—try it now!

The first thing you'll notice is that the Unused Photos section is empty (see Figure 6-5). That's because all the photos are currently in the slideshow. Just drag a few of the slides out of the slideshow and drop them into the Unused Photos column; then, you'll have something more like Figure 6-6.

Filtering by Category

Displaying all unused photos might seem acceptable right now, but we have only nine photos. If there were 900, it would quickly become unusable. So, our final feature in this chapter will be to display only the unused photos in a particular category.

The first thing to do in our controller is to get a list of all categories that can populate the drop-down selection box. Edit *app/controllers/slideshows_controller.rb*, and add this line to the end of the edit method:

```
@all_categories = Category.find(:all, :order=>"name")
```

This line retrieves a list of categories that can populate a drop-down selection box that the user will need to display only those unused photos that are in the selected category.

Now, edit *app/views/slideshows/edit.html.erb*, and add this right after the 'Play this Slideshow' line:

```
<p>
    <label for="category_id">Filter "Unused Photos" on this Category</label><br/>
    <%= collection_select(:category, :id, @all_categories, :id, :long_name) %>
    <%= observe_field(:category_id,
                :frequency => 2.0,
                :update => 'slideshow-photos',
                :url => { :action => 'change_filter'},
                :with => 'category_id' ) %>
</p>
```

The collection_select helper is normally used inside an HTML form, but here we are using it because it conveniently knows how to display a collection in a drop-down box. It will never be submitted as part of a form.

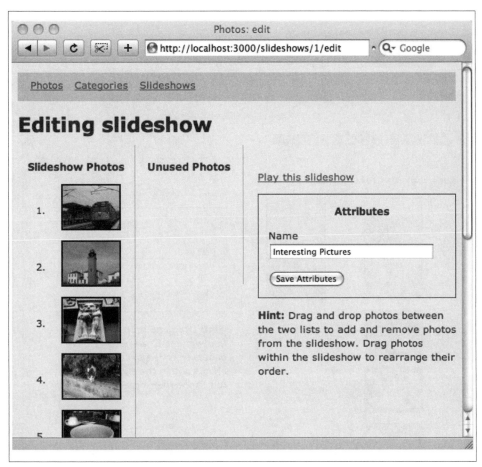

Figure 6-5. Drag-and-drop add and remove

As shown, the `observe_field` helper checks the category drop-down box for changes every two seconds. When a change is detected, an Ajax request is fired off to the `change_filter` method, which returns new HTML (that has been appropriately filtered) to replace the `slideshow-photos` section.

The `Category` model class automatically shows a collection of all photos that are in a particular category. However, we need to get a collection of photos that are in a given category and in all of its child categories.

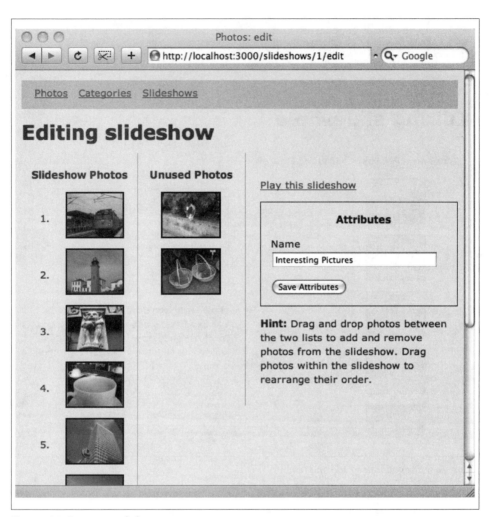

Figure 6-6. Some unused photos

Edit *app/models/category.rb*, and add this method:

```ruby
def photos_including_child_categories
  result = photos.clone
  children.each do |child|
    child.photos_including_child_categories.each do |photo|
      result << photo unless result.include? photo
    end
  end
  result
end
```

This method recursively collects a list of all photos in its own category and all of its child categories. You can use this method to get the list of unused photos to display.

In the meantime, you can edit *app/controllers/slideshows_controller.rb* to add the change_filter method:

```ruby
def change_filter
  category_id = params[:category_id] || 1
  session[:category_id] = category_id
  session[:slideshow] = @slideshow = Slideshow.find(session[:slideshow].id)
  category = Category.find(category_id)
  render :partial => 'unused_photo',
    :collection => category.photos_including_child_categories - @slideshow.photos
end
```

This method stores the chosen category_id in the session hash, retrieves a new list of unused photos, and then renders the photo_picker. If no category was specified, the code arbitrarily chooses category 1, or All.

We're done; we've added category filtering! Fire up your browser and try it (you may need to assign some categories to some unused photos). Now it looks like Figure 6-7.

We've come a long way in a very short time. With fewer than 200 lines of code, we've added drag-and-drop capability to add and reorder slides. We've also added the core capability to actually show a slideshow. Ajax made our application much easier to use and more attractive. Next, we'll look into testing this application. Hang on—the application is almost done.

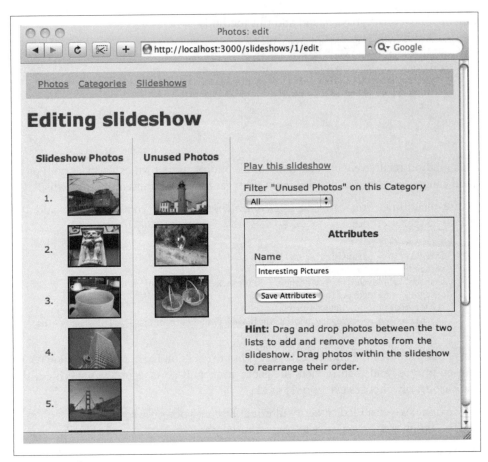

Figure 6-7. Filtering on categories

## CHAPTER 7

Testing

These days, you probably always write automated tests for all your code...or feel guilty for skipping them. Dynamically typed languages such as Ruby don't have a compile step that can catch errors, as Java or C++ does, so Rails makes automated testing a priority. In Rails, testing is not some feature based on a buzzword that was bolted on afterward. Testing has been built-in from the very beginning. Rails was designed to be testable and to produce applications that are testable. It is so easy to create automated tests that you *should* feel guilty if you don't!

We've come this far with our Photo Share web application, but we haven't yet created any tests. Typically, you'll create tests as you go. In truth, skipping the tests was deliberate. We decided to introduce core Rails concepts first without muddying the waters with tests. But now it is time to rectify that situation and start adding tests to our application. So, let's skip the guilt and code some tests.

Background

Rails encourages you to create a well-tested application by actively generating default test cases, fixtures, and helpers for three different types of tests: unit tests for models, functional tests for your controllers, and integration tests for your whole application. Each time you use `script/generate` to create your model, Rails creates a skeleton unit test, fixture, and helper. When you generate a controller, Rails creates a functional test.

Keep in mind that Rails uses an environment and a database dedicated to testing. The database tables will be reset before each new test run, and the environment uses test-friendly configuration. The whole testing framework is Ruby's `Test::Unit`, which we'll discuss in the next section.

Ruby's Test::Unit

Ruby uses a testing framework known as `Test::Unit` (sometimes referred to as *test/unit*) to run your application's tests. `Test::Unit` is similar to the `xUnit` frameworks that you find in other programming languages, like JUnit for Java or NUnit for .NET. Any testing framework uses the same fundamental flow. With any test case, you do the following:

- *Set up the preconditions for the test.* Rails will give you some help here by setting up a database with fixtures that have sample data you define.

- *Use your application.* You'll write code to exercise your application.

- *Compare the result to what you expected to happen.* You will use assertions to make these comparisons.

To say it another way, testing is about stimulus and response. You stimulate your code and observe the response, over and over. If the response is what you expect, the test passes. Otherwise, the test fails. Here's a simple test for a few arithmetic operations in Ruby:

```
require 'test/unit'

class NumberTest < Test::Unit::TestCase

  def test_should_add_two_numbers
    result = 4 + 4          # Use the code
    assert_equal 8, result    # Measure your results against your expectations
  end

  def test_should_divide_two_numbers
    result = 11 / 2          # Use the code
    assert_equal 5.5, result  # Measure your results against your expectations
  end

end
```

In this case, the code being tested is the base Ruby libraries for two math operators, division and addition. Each test exercises some code and then makes an assertion about the expected result. An assertion is like a statement of fact: when you write the line of code assert_equal 8, result, you are saying, "At this point in the program's execution, I believe that the value of result is 8." When Test::Unit runs this test, all of the tests in the individual methods will execute independently, in an arbitrary order. Here's the result (in this case, run from the TextMate editor):

```
Loaded suite /Users/batate/testunit/number_test
Started
.F
Finished in 0.088725 seconds.

  1) Failure:
test_should_divide_two_numbers:12
<5.5> expected but was
<5>.

2 tests, 2 assertions, 1 failures, 0 errors
```

In fact, many developers like to run tests from within their editors or development environments so they can sanity-check their code as they create it. You can also run the tests by just executing the file: `ruby number_test.rb`. You can see that one of the assertions failed! We expected a floating point response, but got a rounded integer. `Test::Unit` flagged the problem and reported a testing failure. You can fix the problem by changing the assertion to `assert_equal 5, result`.

`Test::Unit` will help you organize your test cases, too. You should think of your tests as small independent units. Each *.rb* file has a group of related tests. Each method has a test that can stand on its own. `Test::Unit` will organize tests like this:

- An *assertion* is a single line of code that evaluates an expression and tests the results against an expected value. For example, you might assert that a password is at least six characters long; failing an assertion fails the associated test.

- A *test* is a method, whose name begins with `test_`, that contains a number of related assertions that, when taken together, test one small piece of your application. For example, `test_should_reject_disallowed_passwords` might contain assertions that verify that bad passwords are rejected (such as a password that is too short, contains all spaces, or is the word "password").

- A *test case* class is a subclass of `Test::Unit::TestCase` that contains a collection of test methods designed to test a broader area of your application. For our Photo Share application, we will have a test case class that tests the `Category` model and another that tests the `photos_controller`.

- A *test suite* is a collection of test cases. When you run a test suite, it executes the tests in each test case that it contains. You won't need to use this with Rails applications because Rails handles the task of running all your test cases. Rails will organize test groupings into unit tests for your models, functional tests for your controllers, and integration tests for your entire application.

`Test::Unit` provides many assertions you can use, and Rails throws in a few more. Table 7-1 shows the main ones. Most assert methods take an optional message parameter. If a message is included, then that message is displayed if its assertion fails.

Table 7-1. Commonly used assertions

Assertion	Description
`assert( boolean, [msg] )`	Passes if boolean is true
`assert_equal( expected, actual, [msg] )`	Passes if expected == actual
`assert_not_equal( expected, actual, [msg] )`	
`assert_match( pattern, string, [msg] )`	Passes if string =~ pattern
`assert_no_match( pattern, string, [msg] )`	

Assertion	Description
assert_nil(object, [msg])	Passes if object == nil
assert_not_nil(object, [msg])	
assert_instance_of(class, object, [msg])	Passes if object.class == class
assert_kind_of(class, object, [msg])	Passes if object.kind_of?(class)
assert_raise(Exception, ...) {block}	Passes if the block raises (or doesn't raise) one of the listed exceptions
assert_nothing_raised(Exception, ...) {block}	

You can define two special methods in your test case class: **setup** and **teardown**. Before each test method is executed, **test::unit** calls **setup** to let you set up the environment for each test. You can open a database connection, load test data, and so on. Likewise, immediately after each test method returns, **teardown** is called to clean up and release any resources acquired by **setup**. Make sure you understand **Test::Unit** will call setup and teardown for every test in a file. Running the following program:

```ruby
require 'test/unit'

class NumberTest < Test::Unit::TestCase

  def setup
    puts "\nSetting up"
  end

  def test_something
    puts "Runnning test one"
  end

  def test_another_thing
    puts "Running test two"
  end

  def teardown
    puts "Tearing down\n"
  end

end
```

would produce the following results:

```
Loaded suite /Users/batate/testunit/number_test
Started

Setting up
Running test two
Tearing down

.
Setting up
Runnning test one
Tearing down

.
```

```
Finished in 0.000303 seconds.

2 tests, 0 assertions, 0 failures, 0 errors
```

Notice a couple of things. First, `Test::Unit` calls `setup` and `teardown` twice each. Second, you can't assume the order of the test case. Our code expected the tests to run sequentially, but no dice. Keep those two things in mind, and you'll be well on your way to mastering testing.

Testing in Rails

Rails extends the `Test::Unit` framework to include new assertion methods that are specific to web applications and to the Rails framework. Rails also provides explicit higher-level support for testing by including a consistent method for loading test data and a mechanism for running different types of tests.

Unit Tests, Functional Tests, and Integration Tests

You've already seen that Rails generates unit and functional tests. You've also noticed us mention integration tests. We're going to walk you through some basic tests of each type. Look at your Photo Share application's directory tree, and you'll find that it contains a *test* subdirectory. All tests reside under this *test* subdirectory, which has several subdirectories of its own:

unit
> Holds all unit tests

functional
> Holds all functional tests

integration
> Holds all integration tests

fixtures
> Contains sample data for all tests

In fact, you've already been using test fixtures to build common, repeatable test data that you'll use to take your application through a test drive. Take a look at *test/unit*, and you'll see that it already contains *category_test.rb*, *photo_test.rb*, *slide_test.rb*, and *slideshow_test.rb*. They are test case skeletons created by Rails when we generated our model classes. But before you can start filling out these skeleton test files, you first need to understand Rails' environments and fixtures.

Environments

We software developers have always distinguished between code running in some form of development mode versus production mode. Development mode usually offers features such as active debugging, logging, and array bounds checking. These all add unnecessary overhead, so you should normally strip those conveniences out of your delivered production code.

This distinction of development versus production has often been informal and ad hoc. As introduced in Chapter 2, Rails formalizes this practice using what it calls *environments*. Rails comes with three predefined environments: development, test, and production. You can also define new environments if you like, such as an environment for staging.

Each environment can have its own database and runtime settings. For example, in production mode, you usually want as much caching as possible to maximize performance, but in development mode, you want all caching disabled so that you can make a change and then immediately see it work. The predefined Rails environments have the default settings that make sense for each environment.

There are several ways to tell Rails what environment to use:

- Set the operating system environment variable `RAILS_ENV` to `'development'`, `'production'`, or `'test'`.

- Specify the environment value in *config/environment.rb* with a line of Ruby code like this: `ENV['RAILS_ENV'] = 'production'`. Some developers occasionally use this technique when they are going to be using an environment other than development for an extended period of time without running tests, such as when I'm working on caching or benchmarking with a custom environment.

- Use the -e option on the `script/server` script to start the Mongrel server. For example, `script/server -e production` starts the web server in production mode. Development mode is the default.

- Most often, you'll use command switches in the commands you're using. You can type `script/console` production to load the production environment for the console. You can type `script/server --environment=production` to start your server in production mode. For Rake tasks, you can type `rake RAILS_ENV=test ...rake task...` to run a `rake` command against the test environment. Check the documentation for your script or command to find the specific option you need.

Take a look at Photo Share application's *config/environments* directory, and you will find three files: *development.rb*, *test.rb*, and *production.rb*. Each file contains the settings for its environment. These default environments are pretty well thought out, and it is unlikely that you will need to change them. But as you've already seen, you should change the database settings for each environment in `database.yml`. We're going to live with the defaults, and SQLite will create a database if it doesn't exist. If you're using another database engine, you'll need to create a test database now.

If we're using SQLite, Rails will build the database structure before each test run. If you're using another database engine, you can use a built-in feature of Rails to clone the database schema from the production database to the test database. Open a console window, navigate to the root directory of the Photo Share application, and run the command:

```
>rake db:test:clone
```

Rails will create a test database from *schema.rb*. In either case, we'll use Rails fixtures to put a clean set of data into these tables.

Fixtures

Fixtures contain test data that Rails loads into your models before executing each test. You create your fixture data in the *test/fixtures* directory, and they can be in CSV (comma-separated value) or YAML (YAML Ain't Markup Language) format.

The Great Fixture Debate

Though they are a built-in part of Rails, test fixtures are not universally accepted as the best way of creating test objects. Two distinct camps have emerged. One camp believes that it is important to keep tests DRY (Don't Repeat Yourself). The other camp believes it's more important for tests to maintain isolation. Tying multiple tests to the same data—and tying one test fixture to another—can make your tests harder to maintain.

If you believe that tests should be as DRY as possible, fixtures can help if you design them well. Fixtures allow you to create one common set of data that can be used for all tests. The danger is that you can wind up creating dependencies across your test cases. If one test case counts the number of rows in the database for a table to verify that a row was deleted, adding a new fixture will break your tests. Also, you can try too hard to share data across tests. You should be careful to use fixtures in such a way that it's easy to add test data without impacting other tests. You should also create additional fixtures to support your tests as you need to instead of forcing your tests to use data that does not quite fit.

If you believe that creating isolated tests is more important, you might instead choose an alternative way to manage your test objects. For example, you might create objects in each test, perhaps with a private method, in setup, or in a helper. This approach can force you to work harder to write each test, and thus reduce the total number of tests that you write.

In truth, both isolation and DRY-ness are important in your tests. There is a natural trade-off between the two. Smart people have succeeded and failed with each of these approaches. Both can work. In this book, we're going to use fixtures because that's the testing strategy that's built into Rails. Who knows? Soon, we may be using an alternative strategy as Rails testing evolves.

YAML is the preferred format because it is so simple and readable, consisting mostly of keyword/value pairs. CSV files are useful when you have existing data in a database or spreadsheet that you can export to CSV format. CSV files are useful when you already have input data in that format. You've already seen fixtures in previous chapters. Let's review what a typical fixture might look like:

```
photo_1:
  id: 1
  filename: train.jpg
  thumbnail: train_t.jpg
  description: My ride to work

photo_2:
  id: 2
  filename: lighthouse.jpg
  thumbnail: lighthouse_t.jpg
  description: I take dates here all the time
...
```

In Rails 2, IDs are optional. Remember: YAML is sensitive to whitespace, so be sure to use spaces instead of tabs, and eliminate any trailing spaces or tabs. The first line of each fixture is a name that is assigned to that fixture. You'll use these names in your test cases to quickly refer to a single fixture with some predefined helpers. The remaining lines are keyword/value pairs, one for each column in the database table.

When you execute a test file (assuming you have the default `transactional_fixtures` set up in your testing environment), Rails will load the fixtures once when the file loads, and will issue a rollback after each test. The rollback will undo any changes that your test case made to your database.

Now that we have a test database and some fixtures, we can actually start writing some tests.

Unit tests

In Rails, unit tests are for testing your models. The file *test/unit/photo_test.rb*, for example, is where to create tests to test the `Photo` model. Rails created a skeleton of this file when we created the model. It currently looks like this:

```
require 'test_helper'

class PhotoTest < Test::Unit::TestCase
  # Replace this with your real tests.
  def test_truth
    assert true
  end
end
```

Let's walk through the code a line at a time:

`require 'test_helper'`
> The helper *test_helper.rb* activates the Rails environment so that your tests are ready to run. It's also a common anchor point for functions that will assist your testing. Later, you'll use this file to add a helper that will help you exercise all of the associations on a model.

```
class PhotoTest < Test::Unit::TestCase
```
This code makes the PhotoTest class a subclass of Test::Unit::TestCase, as is required for running tests using Test::Unit.

```
fixtures :photos
```
This code tells Rails to load the *test/fixtures/photos.yml* test fixture. You can load multiple fixtures in one statement like this: `fixtures :photos, :categories, slideshows`.

It's finally time to create and run our first test. Edit *test/unit/photo_test.rb*, and then add this code in the place of the `test_truth` test:

```
fixtures :photos

def test_photo_count
  assert_equal 3, Photo.count
end
```

If you wanted to, you could run all tests with `rake`, like this:

```
rake test:units
```

Instead, you'll often want to run a test on an island. You can call the test directly with Ruby, or from your favorite development environment. Try running the specific test we just built. This test is going to fail because it is asserting that the Photo database table contains three rows, but *photos.yml* contains nine. Let's try it and see. Open a command prompt, navigate to the root directory of our Photo Share application, and run this command:

```
>ruby -Itest test/unit/photo_test.rb
```

Itest stands for Island Test. You should see the following output:

```
Started
.F..
Finished in 0.313 seconds.

  1) Failure:
test_photo_count(PhotoTest) [./test/unit/photo_test.rb:7]:
<3> expected but was
<9>.

5 tests, 5 assertions, 1 failures, 0 errors
```

Remember that the *test/units* directory contains four test files (even though we have modified only one of them), so this test ran all four. As expected, our test failed. Let's fix that:

```
def test_should_find_nine_photos
  assert_equal 9, Photo.count
end
```

When you run the unit tests, you get something like the following (which may vary based on your environment):

```
Started
....
Finished in 0.359 seconds.

5 tests, 5 assertions, 0 failures, 0 errors
```

You know that fixtures are used to populate our database tables. But you can also individually access each fixture's data using the fixture's name.* `photos(:photo_1)` returns an Active Record `Photo` with the data in the fixture, so `photos(:photo_1).id` returns the value of the `id` property (which is 1). You will often use the fixtures helper to create your test objects, like this:

```
photo = photos(:photo_1)
```

Retrieving the `train_photo` object from the database by name is the equivalent to retrieving it by `id`:

```
photo = Photo.find(1)
```

Let's use this feature to add another test to *test/unit/photo_test.rb*:

```
def test_should_load_photo_attributes
  assert_equal 1, photos(:photo_1).id
  assert_equal photos(:photo_1), Photo.find(1)
  assert_equal 2, photos(:photo_2).id
  assert_equal Photo.find(2), photos(:photo_2)
end
```

When you run the unit tests, you get:

```
Started
.....
Finished in 0.359 seconds.

6 tests, 9 assertions, 0 failures, 0 errors
```

Typically, you don't want to use test cases that count fixtures, because the number of fixtures will often change. Let's build a better test. If you need to count rows (for example, to make sure an item was created or destroyed), you can use an assertion called `assert_difference` to make sure that the right number of rows were created or destroyed. Replace the test called `test_should_find_nine_photos` with these two, which make sure a photo gets created and deleted:

```
def test_should_delete_one_photo
  assert_difference 'Photo.count', -1 do
    photos(:photo_1).destroy
  end
end

def test_should_create_one_photo
  assert_difference 'Photo.count' do
    Photo.create(:filename => 'armadillo.jpg', :thumbnail => 'armadillo_t.jpg')
```

---

* Only the YAML format allows you to name a fixture, so if you use the CSV format, you will not be able to do this.

```
      end
    end
```

The `assert_difference` assertion takes an expression in the form of a string, a difference in the form of an integer, and a code block. The expression should return an `Integer`. `assert_difference` executes the expression, runs the code block, and then executes the expression again. If the difference between the before and after expression is the same as the number you specified (1 is the default), the assertion passes. If not, the assertion fails. In the case of the previous test, we want the test to fail unless the count of photos is reduced by one when you delete a photo. Similarly, the second test should fail unless creating a photo increases the count of photos by one.

Often, you'll want to make sure you've got the syntax for all of your association macros right. You can add a test helper to *test/test_helper.rb* that uses Active Record's built-in reflection to exercise all of the association macros such as `has_many :slides` in Photo. Add this method to the bottom of *test/test_helper.rb* (with thanks to Chad Humphries):

```
def assert_working_associations(m=nil)
  m ||= self.class.to_s.sub(/Test$/, '').constantize
  @m = m.new
  m.reflect_on_all_associations.each do |assoc|
    assert_nothing_raised("#{assoc.name} caused an error") do
      @m.send(assoc.name, true)
    end
  end
  true
end
```

Based on the name of the test file, this helper infers the name of the model. Then, the method uses Active Record's feature called `reflect_on_all_associations` to return an array with each of the associations on the model. `association.name` has the name of the instance variable that the association adds to the model. (For example, the Photo class adds `slides` from `has_many :slides`, and `categories` from `has_and_belongs_to_many :categories`.) Next, the method uses `send` to call the added association.

You can see a new assertion called `assert_nothing_raised`. That assertion will fail the test if any exception is raised. Normally, the test would fail with an error if an exception were raised, but `assert_nothing_raised` makes it clear that your code is testing for exceptions. Now, you can add a test case to *test/units/photo_test.rb* like this:

```
def test_should_have_working_associations
  assert_working_associations
end
```

The code you added to your helper will reflect on all associations, attempt to exercise them with a `send`, and fail the test if the association raises an exception. Run your tests for this result:

```
........
Finished in 0.174765 seconds.

8 tests, 12 assertions, 0 failures, 0 errors
```

With our guilt suitably assuaged, let's move on to functional tests.

Functional tests

In Rails, you'll use functional tests to exercise one feature, or function, in your controllers. Functional and integration tests check the responses to web commands, called *http requests*. In this section, we'll work on functional tests for the **photos** controller.

We originally created our **photos** controller by generating scaffolding for it. When you generate scaffolding for a database table, Rails creates a remarkably complete set of functional tests:

```ruby
require 'test_helper'

class PhotosControllerTest < ActionController::TestCase
  def test_should_get_index
    get :index
    assert_response :success
    assert_not_nil assigns(:photos)
  end

  def test_should_get_new
    get :new
    assert_response :success
  end

  def test_should_create_photo
    assert_difference('Photo.count') do
      post :create, :photo => { }
    end

    assert_redirected_to photo_path(assigns(:photo))
  end

  def test_should_show_photo
    get :show, :id => photos(:one).id
    assert_response :success
  end

  def test_should_get_edit
    get :edit, :id => photos(:one).id
    assert_response :success
  end

  def test_should_update_photo
    put :update, :id => photos(:one).id, :photo => { }
    assert_redirected_to photo_path(assigns(:photo))
  end

  def test_should_destroy_photo
```

```
    assert_difference('Photo.count', -1) do
      delete :destroy, :id => photos(:one).id
    end

    assert_redirected_to photos_path
  end
end
```

These tests are in the file *test/functional/photos_controller_test.rb* and cover the full range of CRUD operations. The Rails-generated functional tests for our other controllers are very similar.

First, let's take a little bit of time to understand the Rails testing strategy for functional tests. As you know, all automated testing exercises code and then check the result. With functional tests, you will exercise the code through simulating HTTP calls. You'll call HTTP PUT, GET, DELETE, and POST methods just as you did in the console in Chapter 2. Then, you'll look at the result of that call. The result might be an HTTP success, redirect, or error, but if your code is working correctly, you shouldn't get errors. After calling an HTTP method, you'll use `assert_response` to check the response and symbols to check the HTTP return codes.

You can run the functional tests with the command `rake test:functionals`:

```
.EEF.EEEEE..EE.EE..EE.EE..EE
Finished in 0.332066 seconds.

  1) Error:
test_should_destroy_category(CategoriesControllerTest):
StandardError: No fixture with name 'one' found for table 'categories'
...

  2) Error:
test_should_get_edit(CategoriesControllerTest):
StandardError: No fixture with name 'one' found for table 'categories'
...

  3) Failure:
test_should_get_index(CategoriesControllerTest)
    [./test/functional/categories_controller_test.rb:7:in 'test_should_get_index'
...

  4) Error:
test_should_show_category(CategoriesControllerTest):
StandardError: No fixture with name 'one' found for table 'categories'
...

  5) Error:
test_should_update_category(CategoriesControllerTest):
StandardError: No fixture with name 'one' found for table 'categories'
...

  6) Error:
test_should_create_photo(PhotosControllerTest):
ActionView::TemplateError: You have a nil object when you didn't expect it!
```

```
You might have expected an instance of Array.
The error occurred while evaluating nil.map
    On line #4 of photos/new.html.erb

    1: <h1>New photo</h1>
    2:
    3: <% form_for(@photo) do |f| %>
    4: <%= render :partial => 'form', :locals => { :f => f } %>
    5:    <p>
    6:      <%= f.submit "Create" %>
    7:    </p>

    vendor/rails/actionpack/lib/action_view/helpers/form_options_helper.rb:206:in
    'options_from_collection_for_select'
...
    /Library/Ruby/Gems/1.8/gems/rake-0.8.1/lib/rake/rake_test_loader.rb:5

  7) Error:
test_should_destroy_photo(PhotosControllerTest):
StandardError: No fixture with name 'one' found for table 'photos'
...

  8) Error:
test_should_get_edit(PhotosControllerTest):
StandardError: No fixture with name 'one' found for table 'photos'
...

  9) Error:
test_should_show_photo(PhotosControllerTest):
StandardError: No fixture with name 'one' found for table 'photos'
...

 10) Error:
test_should_update_photo(PhotosControllerTest):
StandardError: No fixture with name 'one' found for table 'photos'
...

 11) Error:
test_should_destroy_slide(SlidesControllerTest):
StandardError: No fixture with name 'one' found for table 'slides'
...

 12) Error:
test_should_get_edit(SlidesControllerTest):
StandardError: No fixture with name 'one' found for table 'slides'
...

 13) Error:
test_should_show_slide(SlidesControllerTest):
StandardError: No fixture with name 'one' found for table 'slides'
...

 14) Error:
test_should_update_slide(SlidesControllerTest):
StandardError: No fixture with name 'one' found for table 'slides'
```

```
...
    15) Error:
test_should_destroy_slideshow(SlideshowsControllerTest):
StandardError: No fixture with name 'one' found for table 'slideshows'
...

    16) Error:
test_should_get_edit(SlideshowsControllerTest):
StandardError: No fixture with name 'one' found for table 'slideshows'
...

    17) Error:
test_should_show_slideshow(SlideshowsControllerTest):
StandardError: No fixture with name 'one' found for table 'slideshows'
...

    18) Error:
test_should_update_slideshow(SlideshowsControllerTest):
StandardError: No fixture with name 'one' found for table 'slideshows'
...

28 tests, 21 assertions, 1 failures, 17 errors
rake aborted!
Command failed with status (1): [/System/Library/Frameworks/Ruby.framework/...]

(See full trace by running task with --trace)
```

You know that the Photo Share application was not coded by drunk monkeys, but you still see way too many errors. Our tests are simply out of date. Those tests worked perfectly fine when they were first created, but since that time, we have made some changes to the code and the fixtures of the generated code. Now, we need to fix these tests. For the purposes of this chapter, we are going to get the photo controller's functional tests working to give you enough understanding to fix the others yourself. We'll provide an enhanced example with full coverage online at *http://www.oreilly.com/catalog/9780596522001*.

Because you can assign every photo to one or more categories, a lot of the photo controller code also works with categories. But we don't yet load the category fixtures.

Edit *test/functional/photos_controller_test.rb,* and add this line to the beginning of the class definition for `PhotosControllerTest`:

```
fixtures :photos, :categories, :categories_photos
```

Let's try running our functional tests. From the base directory of our Photo Share application, run this command:

```
$ ruby -Itest test/functional/photos_controller_test.rb
Loaded suite test/functional/photos_controller_test
Started
EEE..EE
Finished in 0.480665 seconds.
```

```
  1) Error:
test_should_create_photo(PhotosControllerTest):
ActionView::TemplateError: You have a nil object when you didn't expect it!
You might have expected an instance of Array.
The error occurred while evaluating nil.map
    On line #4 of photos/new.html.erb

    1: <h1>New photo</h1>
    2:
    3: <% form_for(@photo) do |f| %>
    4: <%= render :partial => 'form', :locals => { :f => f } %>
    5:   <p>
    6:     <%= f.submit "Create" %>
    7:   </p>

    vendor/rails/actionpack/lib/action_view/helpers/form_options_helper.rb:206:in
    'options_from_collection_for_select'
    ...
    test/functional/photos_controller_test.rb:38

  2) Error:
test_should_destroy_photo(PhotosControllerTest):
StandardError: No fixture with name 'one' found for table 'photos'
    ...

  3) Error:
test_should_get_edit(PhotosControllerTest):
StandardError: No fixture with name 'one' found for table 'photos'
    ...

  4) Error:
test_should_show_photo(PhotosControllerTest):
StandardError: No fixture with name 'one' found for table 'photos'
    ...

  5) Error:
test_should_update_photo(PhotosControllerTest):
StandardError: No fixture with name 'one' found for table 'photos'
    ...
7 tests, 3 assertions, 0 failures, 5 errors
```

Hmmm: that wasn't exactly error-free; there were five test errors. Let's see what's wrong with the first test, called test_should_create_photo:

```
def test_should_create_photo
  assert_difference('Photo.count') do
    post :create, :photo => { }
  end

  assert_redirected_to photo_path(assigns(:photo))
end
```

You've seen the method assert_difference before. Inside of the assert_difference code block is the expected HTTP command of POST. With Rails PUTs or POSTs, you can pass the form parameters within a hash map. You see that this test case does a

POST to :create with an empty hash for the photo. That hash has the attributes from the form. But wait a minute. Look again at the Photo model. There's a validation:

```
class Photo < ActiveRecord::Base
  has_many :slides
  has_and_belongs_to_many :categories

  validates_presence_of :filename

  named_scope :with_filetype_jpg, :conditions => "filename like '%.jpg'"
  named_scope :with_thumbnail, :conditions => "thumbnail not null and thumbnail != ''"
  named_scope :with_filetype,
    lambda {|ftype| { :conditions => ["filename like ?", "%.#{ftype}"] } }
end
```

That makes sense. No photo is created because the test code does not specify a filename. Add a valid hash to the *test/functional/photos_controller_test.rb* file, like this:

```
...
  def test_should_create_photo
    assert_difference('Photo.count') do
      post :create, :photo => { :filename => 'testfilename.jpg' }
    end

    assert_redirected_to photo_path(assigns(:photo))
  end
```

Run a single test to make sure it works:

```
$ ruby -Itest test/functional/photos_controller_test.rb -n test_should_create_photo
Loaded suite test/functional/photos_controller_test
Started
.
Finished in 0.237293 seconds.

1 tests, 3 assertions, 0 failures, 0 errors
```

You can see that the test runs. A quick look at the test errors shows that the other issues are all fixture issues. Look at the test called test_should_show_photo. You'll see the line get :show, :id => photos(:one).id, which passes the id for the photo with a fixture called :one. But wait. The fixtures all have names that we've created instead of the names that Rails generated. A quick peek into test/fixtures/photos.yml reveals a fixture named photo_1. You can replace :one with :photo_1 everywhere in *test/functional/ photos_controller_test* that it appears, four occurrences in all.

Then, you can run all of the tests with ruby -Itest test/functional/photos_control ler_test.rb:

```
$ ruby -Itest test/functional/photos_controller_test.rb
Loaded suite test/functional/photos_controller_test
Started
.......
Finished in 0.242838 seconds.

7 tests, 13 assertions, 0 failures, 0 errors
```

All of the tests ran! Let's take a deeper look at some of the individual functional tests. Often, you'll want to make sure that a controller assigns a value to an instance variable. You can look at the test called `test_should_get_index` and see a good example. This test should verify that Rails successfully renders its page, and that it assigns an instance variable called `photos`. Here's the code:

```
def test_should_get_index
  get :index
  assert_response :success
  assert_not_nil assigns(:photos)
end
```

The magic here is in the assertion `assert_not_nil assigns(:photos)`. The `assigns()` method takes a symbol and returns the value of that instance variable.

While we're working with these tests, take a look at some of the test cases that illustrate a redirect. Take another look at `test_should_create_photo` again. You'll see the assertion `assert_redirected_to photo_path(assigns(:photo))`. This test uses `assigns` to return the value for `@photo`, and then uses that code to make sure that Rails takes the redirect that's specified in the `photos_controller`. The test case uses one of the named routes created by Rails automatically.

Rails adds a number of assertions to `Test::Unit` that you may find helpful.

The functional tests are only a starting point. The next step is to make sure that the tests execute each line of code. To do so, you'll need a metric called code coverage.

Test Coverage

By using a plug-in called `RCov`, you can always tell exactly what lines of code within your application are covered. To use it, you'll have to make a few modifications to the project. First, you'll need to install the gem, and the Rails plug-in for coverage. As usual, omit the `sudo` on the Windows platform:

```
$ sudo gem install rcov
Password:
Updating metadata for 104 gems from http://gems.rubyforge.org/
.........................................................................
complete
Building native extensions.  This could take a while...
Successfully installed rcov-0.8.1.2.0
1 gem installed
Installing ri documentation for rcov-0.8.1.2.0...
Installing RDoc documentation for rcov-0.8.1.2.0...
lance-carlsons-macbook-pro:photos lancelotcarlson$ script/plugin install
http://svn.codahale.com/rails_rcov
+ ./MIT-LICENSE
+ ./README
+ ./tasks/rails_rcov.rake
```

By default, this tool will measure coverage for all types of tests independently. You will also find it useful to measure the total coverage of all of your tests. To do so, you'll need another rake task. Add the file called *lib/tasks/coverage.rake* to the project, and make it look like this:

```
require 'rcov/rcovtask'

namespace :test do
  desc 'Aggregate code coverage for unit, functional and integration tests'
  Rcov::RcovTask.new(:coverage => 'db:test:prepare') do |t|
    t.libs << "test"
    t.test_files = FileList["test/unit/*_test.rb","test/functional/*_test.rb",
    "test/integration/*_test.rb"]
    t.output_dir = "coverage"
    t.verbose = true
    t.rcov_opts << '--comment --rails --exclude=db/*,lib/*,config/* '
  end
end
```

Now, you can run that rake task with rake test:coverage to produce the following output:

```
rake test:coverage
(in /Users/batate/Documents/uar/src/chapter5/photos)

...

Started
.EEF.EE...........EE..EE..EE..EE
Finished in 1.129406 seconds.

...

33 tests, 36 assertions, 1 failures, 12 errors
```

File	Lines	LOC	COV
app/controllers/application.rb	10	4	100.0%
app/controllers/categories_controller.rb	75	62	43.5%
app/controllers/photos_controller.rb	75	62	80.6%
app/controllers/slides_controller.rb	85	60	43.3%
app/controllers/slideshows_controller.rb	85	60	43.3%
app/helpers/application_helper.rb	3	2	100.0%
app/helpers/categories_helper.rb	2	2	100.0%
app/helpers/photos_helper.rb	2	2	100.0%
app/helpers/slides_helper.rb	2	2	100.0%
app/helpers/slideshows_helper.rb	5	5	100.0%
app/models/category.rb	16	14	100.0%
app/models/person.rb	7	7	100.0%
app/models/photo.rb	11	9	100.0%
app/models/slide.rb	6	5	100.0%
app/models/slideshow.rb	3	3	100.0%
Total	387	299	61.5%

```
+-----------------------------------------------------+-------+-------+--------+
  61.5%   15 file(s)    387 Lines    299 LOC
```

Before you pay attention to the coverage statistics, you'll notice that there are still errors. It's always dangerous to rely on coverage numbers before you've fixed all test errors because errors limit test coverage. We're going to fix them now using the techniques you've already seen. In test/functional/categories_controller_test.rb, we're going to require fixtures with fixtures :categories and replace the fixture name :one with category_1. We also need to change the assert_difference('Category.count', -1) assertion inside of the test_should_destroy_category to assert_difference('Category.count', -7) to account for the fact that a category is a tree, so deleting the root node will delete all of the categories. We also need to change an assertion in test_should_get_index to assert_not_nil assigns(:all_categories) to reflect changes in the controller. Running tests should now show only eight errors and improved coverage.

In SlidesControllerTest, we will require fixtures with fixtures :slides and change the name of the fixture :one to :slide_1 globally in the file. I'll make the same changes to SlideshowsControllerTest, but with fixtures :slideshows and the fixture name :slideshow_1. Now, all tests pass. Running test:coverage gives me better coverage stats:

```
rake test:coverage

...
Loaded suite /opt/local/bin/rcov
Started
..............................
Finished in 0.88623 seconds.

33 tests, 57 assertions, 0 failures, 0 errors
+-----------------------------------------------------+-------+-------+--------+
|                     File                            | Lines |  LOC  |  COV   |
+-----------------------------------------------------+-------+-------+--------+
|app/controllers/application.rb                       |   10  |    4  | 100.0% |
|app/controllers/categories_controller.rb             |   75  |   62  |  80.6% |
|app/controllers/photos_controller.rb                 |   75  |   62  |  80.6% |
|app/controllers/slides_controller.rb                 |   85  |   60  |  80.0% |
|app/controllers/slideshows_controller.rb             |   85  |   60  |  80.0% |
|app/helpers/application_helper.rb                    |    3  |    2  | 100.0% |
|app/helpers/categories_helper.rb                     |    2  |    2  | 100.0% |
|app/helpers/photos_helper.rb                         |    2  |    2  | 100.0% |
|app/helpers/slides_helper.rb                         |    2  |    2  | 100.0% |
|app/helpers/slideshows_helper.rb                     |    5  |    5  | 100.0% |
|app/models/category.rb                               |   16  |   14  | 100.0% |
|app/models/person.rb                                 |    7  |    7  | 100.0% |
|app/models/photo.rb                                  |   11  |    9  | 100.0% |
|app/models/slide.rb                                  |    6  |    5  | 100.0% |
|app/models/slideshow.rb                              |    3  |    3  | 100.0% |
+-----------------------------------------------------+-------+-------+--------+
|Total                                                |  387  |  299  |  83.9% |
```

```
+-----------------------------------------------------------+-------+-------+--------+
  83.9%   15 file(s)   387 Lines   299 LOC
```

Notice that the test coverage is not complete. The four controllers are showing coverage of only 80%. You can see exactly which lines of code are covered by pointing your browser to the file `coverage/index.html`. On OS X, you can type `open coverage/index.html` to get my coverage report, and on Windows, you can type `start coverage/index.html` to do the same if you prefer the command line. Click on the photos controller. You'll see the untested lines in red (for the black-and-white version of what will appear on your screen, see Figure 7-1). You'll see that we don't yet test the error paths for `create` or `update`. That report makes sense because we don't yet have test cases for those error conditions.

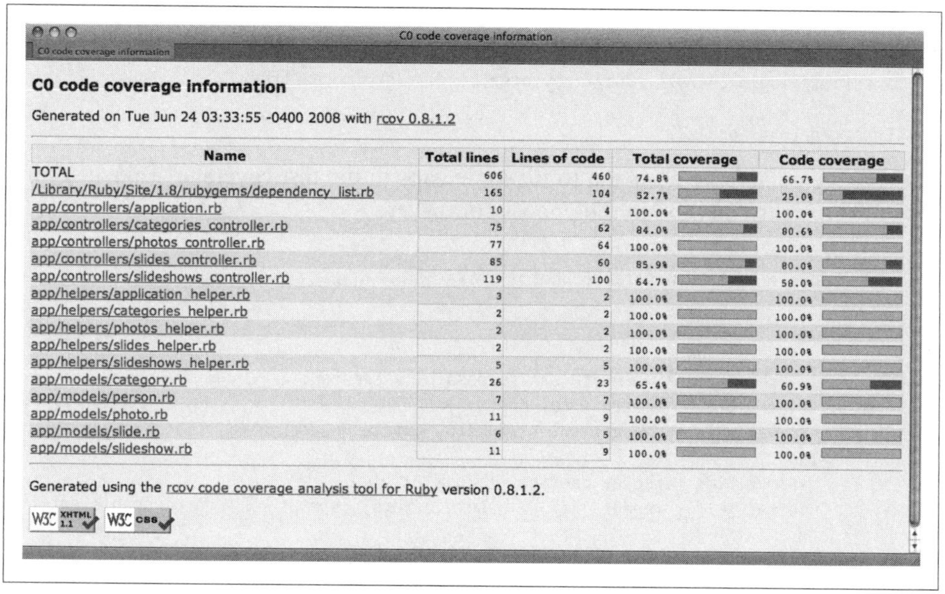

Figure 7-1. Test coverage

Producing the error conditions for photos would not be hard because of the validation on the `Photo` model. In fact, earlier in this chapter, a test failed because it was exercising the failed path unexpectedly; the `post photo` command did not supply a filename. But sometimes, you want to force an error path without physically changing your model. For example, you might want to simulate an error in `save`, but without touching your production code. Doing so requires another plug-in for a technique called mocking. That's the subject of the next section.

Mocking with Mocha

Software testers often substitute *mock objects* for real-world implementations that may be difficult to test or use. Ruby makes mocking easy because you can add a substitute for any method. This technique makes it easy to play "what if" when you are testing. If you wonder what would happen if a test should fail, you could replace the complicated **save** method with a method that does nothing but return **false**.

Rails supports several different mocking frameworks. In this chapter, we're going to use Mocha to change the behavior of some parts of our application to make it easier to test. To install the Mocha gem, do the following:

```
$ sudo gem install mocha
Password:
Successfully installed mocha-0.5.6
1 gem installed
Installing ri documentation for mocha-0.5.6...
Installing RDoc documentation for mocha-0.5.6...
```

Next, install it as a plug-in:

```
$ script/plugin install svn://rubyforge.org/var/svn/mocha/trunk
...
Exported revision 313.
```

Now, we're going to use Mocha to fill some gaps in the test coverage. Take a second look at the **create** method in the photos controller:

```
def create
  @photo = Photo.new(params[:photo])

  respond_to do |format|
    if @photo.save
      flash[:notice] = 'Photo was successfully created.'
      format.html { redirect_to(@photo) }
      format.xml  { render :xml => @photo, :status => :created, :location => @photo }
    else
      format.html { render :action => "new" }
      format.xml  { render :xml => @photo.errors, :status => :unprocessable_entity }
    end
  end
end
```

The uncovered part of this method is the **else** condition of the **if @photo.save** statement. To cover this statement, you will need to make the **save** method fail. We'll use Mocha to do so. Add a test case to *test/functional/photos_controller_test* that looks like this:

```
def test_should_gracefully_fail_and_render_new
  Photo.any_instance.expects(:save).returns(false)
end
```

This single-line test is not yet complete. This test replaces the **save** method on all instances of **Photo** with a method that does nothing but return **false**. That behavior is exactly what we'll want because it will eventually force the **photos** controller to execute the uncovered code in **create**. Run the test with **ruby -Itest test/functional/photos_controller_test.rb -n test_should_gracefully_fail_and_render_new**. You'll get this output:

```
Started
F
Finished in 0.109661 seconds.

  1) Failure:
test_should_gracefully_fail_and_render_new(PhotosControllerTest)
    [test/functional/photos_controller_test.rb:49:in
    'test_should_gracefully_fail_and_render_new'
...
not all expectations were satisfied
unsatisfied expectations:
- expected exactly once, not yet invoked: #<AnyInstance:Photo(id: integer,
filename: string, thumbnail: string,
description: string, created_at: datetime, updated_at: datetime)>.save(any_parameters)
```

Notice that the test failed, even though you have no assertions! Instead, you see an additional feature of mock objects: if the expected mocked method is never called, the test fails. In this case, our test never causes **save** to fire, so the test fails. Now, you can add more meat to the test:

```
def test_should_gracefully_fail_and_render_new
  Photo.any_instance.expects(:save).returns(false)

  assert_no_difference 'Photo.count' do
    post :create, :photo => { :filename => 'cat.photo' }

    assert_response :success
    assert_template 'new'
  end
end
```

Once again, run the test with `ruby -Itest test/functional/photos_control ler_test.rb -n test_should_gracefully_fail_and_render_new`. Surprise! The test failed. Since generating this test code, we've added additional code to the new form that displays categories, but the categories don't exist when we render new from the create action. Now, our systematic approach to covering all of our code with basic tests is turning up real bugs. You can easily fix the test with this change to *app/controllers/photos_controller.rb*. Set the categories within the create method immediately below the else:

```
def create
  @photo = Photo.new(params[:photo])

  respond_to do |format|
    if @photo.save
      flash[:notice] = 'Photo was successfully created.'
      format.html { redirect_to(@photo) }
      format.xml  { render :xml => @photo, :status => :created,
      :location => @photo }
    else
      @all_categories = Category.find(:all, :order => "name")
      format.html { render :action => "new" }
      format.xml  { render :xml => @photo.errors, :status =>
      :unprocessable_entity }
```

```
      end
    end
  end
```

You can run the test and it passes. This means that all assertions in the test case passed, and that **save** was called exactly once on any instance of **Photo**. You can use the same technique to handle the uncovered edit code. Make the changes noted in *test/functional/photos_controller_test.rb* and *app/controllers/photos_controller.rb* below:

```
def test_should_gracefully_fail_and_render_edit
  Photo.any_instance.expects(:update_attributes).returns(false)

  put :update, :id => photos(:photo_1).id, :photo => { }
  assert_response :success
  assert_template 'edit'
end
```

The previous change adds a test case to test the uncovered portions of the method. It uses a mock object to replace the **update_attributes** method on all instances of **Photo** with a method that returns **false**. Next, we have to make sure that the **update** action correctly sets the **@all_categories** instance variable:

```
def update
  @photo = Photo.find(params[:id])

  respond_to do |format|
    if @photo.update_attributes(params[:photo])
      flash[:notice] = 'Photo was successfully updated.'
      format.html { redirect_to(@photo) }
      format.xml  { head :ok }
    else
      @all_categories = Category.find(:all, :order => "name")
      format.html { render :action => "edit" }
      format.xml  { render :xml => @photo.errors, :status => :unprocessable_entity }
    end
  end
end
```

Now, when you run the full coverage report, you'll see 100% coverage for the PhotosControllerTest:

```
Started
....................................
Finished in 1.160718 seconds.

35 tests, 64 assertions, 0 failures, 0 errors
+----------------------------------------------------+-------+-------+--------+
|                       File                         | Lines |  LOC  |  COV   |
+----------------------------------------------------+-------+-------+--------+
|app/controllers/application.rb                      |    10 |     4 | 100.0% |
|app/controllers/categories_controller.rb            |    75 |    62 |  80.6% |
|app/controllers/photos_controller.rb                |    77 |    64 | 100.0% |
|app/controllers/slides_controller.rb                |    85 |    60 |  80.0% |
|app/controllers/slideshows_controller.rb            |    85 |    60 |  80.0% |
|app/helpers/application_helper.rb                   |     3 |     2 | 100.0% |
```

```
|app/helpers/categories_helper.rb               |    2 |    2 | 100.0% |
|app/helpers/photos_helper.rb                    |    2 |    2 | 100.0% |
|app/helpers/slides_helper.rb                    |    2 |    2 | 100.0% |
|app/helpers/slideshows_helper.rb                |    5 |    5 | 100.0% |
|app/models/category.rb                          |   16 |   14 | 100.0% |
|app/models/person.rb                            |    7 |    7 | 100.0% |
|app/models/photo.rb                             |   11 |    9 | 100.0% |
|app/models/slide.rb                             |    6 |    5 | 100.0% |
|app/models/slideshow.rb                         |    3 |    3 | 100.0% |
+------------------------------------------------+------+------+--------+
|Total                                           |  389 |  301 |  88.0% |
+------------------------------------------------+------+------+--------+
 88.0%   15 file(s)    389 Lines    301 LOC
```

That's more like it. We have 100% coverage for the `PhotosController` code, and we know how to improve the code coverage for the rest. This chapter is already too long, but we should cover the complete list of assertions for Rails tests and do a shallow dive into integration tests.

Assertions and Integration Tests

For the remainder of this chapter, we're going to take a quick look at some of the aspects of the testing framework that we've not seen in detail. We'll list all of the assertions available to you and make a quick pass through integration testing.

Assertions in Rails

Did you notice that functional tests for the photos controller use a lot of assertions that are not part of `Test::Unit`, but seem to be specific to web development (`assert_redirected_to`) and even specific to Rails (`assert_template`)? Rails provides these additional assertions. Table 7-2 shows all of the extra assertions provided by Rails.

Table 7-2. Rails-supplied assertions

Assertion	Description
assert_dom_equal	Asserts that two HTML strings are logically equivalent.
assert_dom_not_equal	Asserts that two HTML strings are not logically equivalent.
assert_generates	Asserts that the provided options can generate the provided path.
assert_select	Uses CSS selector syntax to assert contents of HTML or XML.
assert_recognizes	Asserts that the routing rules successfully parse the given URL path.
assert_redirected_to	Asserts that the response is a redirect to the specified destination.
assert_response	Asserts that the response was the given HTTP status code (or range of status codes).
assert_routing	Asserts that path (URL) and options match both ways.
assert_template	Asserts that the request was rendered with the specified template file.
assert_valid	Asserts that the provided record is valid by active record standards.

Integration Tests

Integration tests were introduced in Rails 1.1. Integration tests are higher-level scenario tests that verify the interactions between the application's actions, across all controllers.

As you might have guessed by now, integration tests live in the *test/integration* directory and are run using the command `rake test:integration`.

Our Photo Share application hasn't yet been developed to the point where integration tests would be useful. Instead, here is a hypothetical integration test to give you a feel for what they are like:

```
require "#{File.dirname(__FILE__)}/../test_helper"

class UserManagementTest < ActionController::IntegrationTest
  fixtures :users, :preferences

  def test_register_new_user
    get "/login"
    assert_response :success
    assert_template "login/index"

    get "/register"
    assert_response :success
    assert_template "register/index"

    post "/register",
        :user_name => "happyjoe",
        :password => "neversad"
    assert_response :redirect
    follow_redirect!
    assert_response :success
    assert_template "welcome"
  end
end
```

This test leads its application through the series of web pages that a new user would go through to register with the site. You can see that the scenario being tested is pretty easy to follow:

1. Send an HTTP GET request for the */login* page. Now, check to see whether the request was successful and whether the response was rendered by the expected template.

2. Simulate the user clicking on the "register" button or link by sending an HTTP GET request for the */register* page. Again, check for the proper response.

3. Simulate the new user filling out and submitting the registration form by sending an HTTP POST request that includes user_name and password field values. Now, verify that the response is a redirect, follow the redirect, and verify that you successfully ended up on the welcome page.

Integration tests can be used to duplicate bugs that have been reported. You'll know when you've fixed the bug because your tests will start succeeding; also, you'll have a test in place that will alert you if the same bug ever reappears.

Selenium

The Rails integration testing framework is not the only available integration testing tool at your disposal. *Selenium* is a testing tool written specifically for web applications. Selenium tests run directly in a browser, just as real applications do, provided it's a modern browser that supports JavaScript. As such, it's an ideal tool for testing the Ajax features of a web application.

You can learn more about Selenium on its home page at *http://www.openqa.org/sele nium/*. IBM's developerWorks has a good article on using Selenium with Ruby on Rails at the following address: *http://www-128.ibm.com/developerworks/java/library/wa-se lenium-ajax/index.html*.

Wrapping Up

Testing concludes our whirlwind tour through the Rails framework. We've barely scratched the surface. Photo Share is not nearly complete. We could have easily added:

- *Security*. This is available with the Rails login generator or one of the other login products. With a security model, you can let each user manage and share her own set of photos, instead of having one community model.
- *Uploading photos*. You need to let the user upload photos by some other means, but Rails provides excellent support for simple tasks such as file uploads.
- *attachment_fu*. This plug-in is excellent for managing file uploads. *attachment_fu* can also create thumbnails for you as your user uploads their photos!
- *Deployment*. We've not even touched on pushing the Photo Share application into production, but good tools such as Capistrano (*http://manuals.rubyonrails.com/read/book/17*) allow one-click deployment and also a one-click reversal of changes.
- *Comments and blogging*. You can allow discussion about slides and slideshows. Simple support isn't difficult, but you can also build in the Typo blogging engine.

We've decided that these changes are beyond the scope of a quick-start book, but this list provides a sample of the community that's rapidly developing behind Rails. After this pass through Photo Share, you will doubtlessly be excited about doing more. In the appendixes that follow, we'll give you another whirlwind tour of what's available and how to find more information.

In Rails, an idea is rapidly crystallizing before our eyes as a real force in this industry, but this phenomenon is unlike anything you've ever seen before. So far, this explosion is happening within the open source community, without major commercial investment, and with an amazing amount of contribution from increasingly diverse contributors. This growth is fueled by a core of smart developers who understand that beautiful software can also be powerful, that useful development environments don't need to come from a corporation, and that real innovation doesn't always take the path you expect. We hope you've experienced a taste of what is to come. The rules are all changing. Welcome to the new game.

Installing Rails

Ruby on Rails makes developing web applications easier and more productive than ever before. Not surprisingly, getting a Ruby on Rails development environment installed is pretty easy as well. But be forewarned: this is a very short appendix because getting started is pretty darn easy.

The best way to get up and running with Rails on Windows is to install everything manually. Using pre-packaged options such as Instant Rails will get you up and running quickly; however, you may not want to be stuck using the versions of MySQL, Apache, and so on, that are included in those bundles.

Windows

Ruby One-Click Installer

The Ruby One-Click Installer is the most popular Ruby Interpreter for Windows. For more details about the Ruby One-Click Installer for Windows, go to the home page at *http://rubyinstaller.rubyforge.org/*:

1. Download and unzip the latest version of the Ruby One-Click Installer ZIP file from *http://rubyforge.org/frs/?group_id=167*.

2. Click through the wizard by clicking Next or I agree, depending on the page. The defaults should work perfectly.

The Ruby One-Click Installer for Windows includes the SciTE text editor with full Ruby syntax highlighting. After installing the One-Click Installer, you can find the SciTE executable at *C:\ruby\scite\SciTE.exe*.

We're not done yet! The One-Click Installer doesn't come with Rails, but getting it is easy.

Ruby on Rails

The One-Click Installer comes with the package management system for Ruby called *gems*. This enables us to install Rails very easily. Here are the steps:

1. Press Start → Run and type **cmd** (without quotes), then press Enter to open up the Command Prompt.

2. Type **gem install rails -y** and press Enter. This could take a while, so don't stress if you don't see output immediately.

3. Type **rails -v** and press Enter to verify that Rails was installed. The output should give you the version of Rails running:

```
C:\Documents and Settings\Lance>rails -v
Rails 2.1.0
```

Mongrel

Though it's not necessary, it is a good idea to install the Mongrel web server. Most likely, you will use it in production, and mirroring your development environment as closely as possible to your production environment will decrease the amount of inconsistencies you will experience when deploying to production. If you've finished installing the Ruby One-Click Installer and still have the Command Prompt open, then follow these steps:

1. Type gem **install mongrel -y** and press Enter. You should get the following output:

```
Select which gem to install for your platform (i386-mswin32)
1. mongrel 1.1.5 (ruby)
2. mongrel 1.1.5 (x86-mswin32-60)
3. mongrel 1.1.5 (java)
4. mongrel 1.1.4 (x86-mswin32-60)
5. mongrel 1.1.4 (ruby)
6. mongrel 1.1.4 (java)
7. Skip this gem
8. Cancel installation
>
```

2. Type 2 and press Enter (or whichever number represents the latest version of Mongrel for mswin32). Your output should look like this:

```
> 2
Successfully installed mongrel-1.1.5-x86-mswin32-60
Successfully installed gem_plugin-0.2.3
Successfully installed cgi_multipart_eof_fix-2.5.0
Installing ri documentation for mongrel-1.1.5-x86-mswin32-60...
Installing ri documentation for gem_plugin-0.2.3...
Installing ri documentation for cgi_multipart_eof_fix-2.5.0...
Installing RDoc documentation for mongrel-1.1.5-x86-mswin32-60...
Installing RDoc documentation for gem_plugin-0.2.3...
Installing RDoc documentation for cgi_multipart_eof_fix-2.5.0...
```

SQLite

Throughout the book we use the simple database engine called SQLite. It's easy to set up to get up and running quickly, but it is not meant for high-traffic websites. You might want to consider MySQL if you need some more power. Below are the steps to getting SQLite set up:

1. Download the latest precompiled binary for Windows here: *http://www.sqlite.org/download.html*.

2. Unzip the ZIP file and copy the *sqlite3.exe* file to *C:\WINDOWS\system*.

3. Inside your Command Prompt, type `sqlite3 -help` and press Enter to verify that SQLite was installed. The output should look something like the following:

```
C:\Documents and Settings\Lance>sqlite3 -help
Usage: sqlite3 [OPTIONS] FILENAME [SQL]
FILENAME is the name of an SQLite database. A new database is created
if the file does not previously exist.
OPTIONS include:
  -init filename       read/process named file
  -echo                print commands before execution
  -[no]header          turn headers on or off
  -bail                stop after hitting an error
  -interactive         force interactive I/O
  -batch               force batch I/O
  -column              set output mode to 'column'
  -csv                 set output mode to 'csv'
  -html                set output mode to HTML
  -line                set output mode to 'line'
  -list                set output mode to 'list'
  -separator 'x'       set output field separator (|)
  -nullvalue 'text'    set text string for NULL values
  -version             show SQLite version
```

4. Now that SQLite is installed, we need to install the adapter. Type gem `install sqlite-ruby` and press Enter. The output should look like this:

```
C:\Documents and Settings\Lance>gem install sqlite-ruby
Select which gem to install for your platform (i386-mswin32)
 1. sqlite-ruby 2.2.3 (ruby)
 2. sqlite-ruby 2.2.3 (mswin32)
 3. sqlite-ruby 2.2.2 (mswin32)
 4. sqlite-ruby 2.2.2 (ruby)
 5. Skip this gem
 6. Cancel installation
>
```

5. Type 2 and press Enter (or type the number that is associated with the latest mswin32 version). Your output should look something like this:

```
> 2
Successfully installed sqlite-ruby-2.2.3-mswin32
Installing ri documentation for sqlite-ruby-2.2.3-mswin32...
Installing RDoc documentation for sqlite-ruby-2.2.3-mswin32...
```

Figure A-1. RadRails

RadRails

If you want more than a simple text editor, then try out the excellent RadRails IDE. RadRails (see Figure A-1) is an Eclipse plug-in and is available as a standalone IDE (Eclipse with the plug-in preinstalled) and as a standard Eclipse plug-in at *http://www.radrails.org*. With RadRails, you get a full IDE, complete with an integrated GUI debugger.

After you install RadRails, you have to configure it to work with your Instant Rails installation:

1. Execute the menu command Window → Preferences.

2. Select Ruby → Installed Interpreters.

3. Click the Add button, and give the new interpreter instance a name (such as "Instant Rails Ruby"); browse to the Ruby executable at *InstantRails/ruby/bin/ruby.exe*, and click OK.

4. While still in the preferences dialog, select Ruby->Ri/rdoc and set the Rdoc and Ri paths to *InstantRails/ruby/bin/rdoc* and *InstantRails/ruby/bin/ri*, respectively. This step lets you use the built-in documentation features of RadRails.

You can create a new skeleton Rails application via the menus with File → New... → Rails → RailsProject.

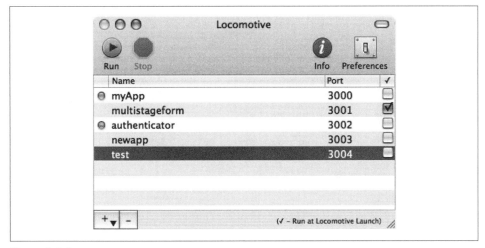

Figure A-2. Locomotive

OS X

The easiest way to get started on OS X is to use Locomotive (see Figure A-2), which is very similar to Instant Rails on Windows, except that it uses the Lighttpd for the web server (instead of Apache) and SQLite for the database (instead of MySQL). For more details about Locomotive, go to its home page at *http://locomotive.raaum.org*.

1. Download Locomotive from *http://sourceforge.net/project/showfiles.php?group_id =146941* (you can also download the "Bundle" version that contains extra libraries, like Rmagick).
2. Simply drag-and-drop the file you just downloaded to your *Applications* folder.
3. To start Locomotive, double-click *Locomotive.app*.

That's all there is to it!

TextMate and RadRails

The commercial text-editor-on-steroids TextMate (see Figure A-3) is very popular with Rails developers on OS X. Locomotive provides some minimal built-in support for TextMate. You can right-click a Rails app in Locomotive and choose to open its directory in TextMate.

TextMate is inexpensive, but not free. You can find out more about TextMate here: *http://macromates.com*.

If you want more than a pumped-up text editor, you'll be happy to know that the excellent RadRails IDE also runs on OS X. See the section "RadRails," earlier in this chapter.

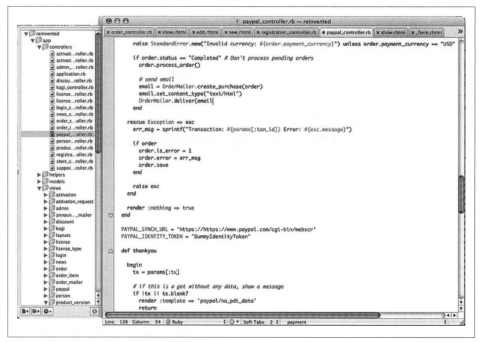

Figure A-3. TextMate

Once installed, you can configure RadRails to work with your Locomotive installation by following the same steps shown earlier in the Windows section of this appendix.

Linux

There is no one simple way to install a Ruby on Rails development environment on Linux distributions. Although the steps may be similar for each distribution, they are different enough that we will just point you to some external instructions. If you don't find your distribution here, try a Google search for "installing ruby on rails on *<your-distro-here>*".

Fedora Core
    http://www.digitalmediaminute.com/howto/fc4rails/

Debian
    http://www.debian-administration.org/articles/329

Gentoo
    http://gentoo-wiki.com/HOWTO_RoR

Ubuntu (Hoary)
    http://paulgoscicki.com/archives/2005/09/ruby-on-rails-on-ubuntu/

Ubuntu (Hoary) using XAMPP

   http://townx.org/ruby_on_rails_on_xampp_with_fastcgi_for_ubuntu_hoary

SUSE

   http://wiki.rubyonrails.org/rails/pages/RailsOnSUSE

Quick Reference

The whole purpose of this book has been to get you up and running quickly with Ruby on Rails. You've learned how the core pieces of Rails work and how to use Rails to build a basic web application. Rails contains more features and capabilities than can be covered in a quick-start book like this. This appendix contains a concise list of the features of Rails with links to more information.

Substantial parts of this quick reference are taken from "What Is Ruby on Rails" by Curt Hibbs,* the "InVisible Ruby On Rails Reference 1.1.2" by InVisible GmbHd,† and the official Ruby on Rails API documentation (*http://api.rubyonrails.com*). This appendix is released under the Creative Commons license (*http://creativecommons.org/licenses/by-sa/2.5/*) and can be downloaded from this book's website: *http://www.oreilly.com/catalog/9780596522001*.

General

Documentation

API for local installation
   gem_server
   http://localhost:8088/
Official Rails API
   http://api.rubyonrails.com
Searchable Rails API
   http://rails.outertrack.com
   http://railshelp.com

---

* "What Is Ruby on Rails" was published at ONLamp.com in October 2005 (*http://www.onlamp.com/pub/a/onlamp/2005/10/13/what_is_rails.html*).

† The "InVisible Ruby On Rails Reference 1.1.2" was released under the Creative Commons license. The original version can be found at *http://blog.invisible.ch/files/rails-reference-1.1.html*.

Ruby documentation
　http://ruby-doc.org

Excellent multi-API documentation
　Includes Ruby, Ruby on Rails, HTML, CSS, JavaScript, DOM, and more: *http://www.gotapi.com*

Supported Web Servers

Mongrel
Lighttpd
nginx
Apache
MS IIS
WEBrick

Learn more: *http://wiki.rubyonrails.org/rails/pages/FAQ#webservers*

Supported Databases

DB2
Firebird
Informix
MySQL
Oracle
PostgreSQL
SQLite
SQL Server
SybaseASA

New drivers are under development, too.

Learn more: *http://wiki.rubyonrails.org/rails/pages/DatabaseDrivers*

Integrated Development Environments (IDEs)

Open Source

Eclipse/RDT
　http://rubyeclipse.sourceforge.net

FreeRIDE
　http://freeride.rubyforge.org

RadRails (built on Eclipse/RDT)
　http://www.radrails.org

RDE (Ruby Development Environment)
    http://homepage2.nifty.com/sakazuki/rde_e.html

Commercial

ArachnoRuby
    http://www.ruby-ide.com/ruby/ruby_ide_and_ruby_editor.php
Komodo
    http://www.activestate.com/Products/Komodo

Editors

Several options
    http://wiki.rubyonrails.org/rails/pages/Editors

Debugging

Logfiles
    Look for the files *development.log*, *test.log*, and *production.log*
Interactive Rails Console
    http://wiki.rubyonrails.com/rails/pages/Console

    http://www.clarkware.com/cgi/blosxom/2006/04/04
Breakpoint
    http://wiki.rubyonrails.com/rails/pages/HowtoDebugWithBreakpoint
Debuggers
    See the IDEs listed earlier in this appendix
Rails debug pop up
    http://www.bigbold.com/snippets/posts/show/697

Create a New Rails Application

    `rails` *app_name*

Options:

`-d=`*xxx* `or --database=`*xxx*
    Specify which database to use (`mysql`, `oracle`, `postgresql`, `sqlite3`, etc.); defaults
    to `mysql`

`-r=`*xxx* `or --ruby-path=`*xxx*
    Specify the path to Ruby; if not set, the scripts use `env` to find Ruby

`-f` *or* `-freeze`
    Freeze Rails into the *vendor/rails* directory

`-v` *or* `-version`
    Show the Rails version number

-h *or* -help
> Show the help message for the **rails** command

Testing

```
rake test                # Test all units and functionals
rake test:functionals    # Run tests for functionals
rake test:integration    # Run tests for integration
rake test:units          # Run tests for units
```

Unit Tests

```
rake test:units
```

Available assertions:

```
assert_kind_of Class, @var  # same class
assert @var                 # not nil
assert_equal 1, @p.id       # equality
@product.destroy
assert_raise(ActiveRecord::RecordNotFound) { Product.find( @product.id ) }
assert_difference 'Photo.count' { Photo.create }
assert_no_difference 'Photo.count { Photo.create(:name => 'invalid name') }
```

Functional Tests

```
rake test:functionals
```

Requests

```
get :action # a get request of the specified action
get :action, :id => 1,
        { session_hash }, # optional session variables
        { flash_hash }    # optional messages in the flash

post :action, :foo => { :value1 => 'abc', :value2 => '123' },
        { :user_id => 17 },
        { :message => 'success' }

get, post, put, delete, head

assert_response :success
# possible parameters are:
#    :success
#    :redirect
#    :missing
#    :error
```

Redirects

```
assert_redirected_to :action => :other_action
assert_redirected_to :controller => 'foo', :action => 'bar'
assert_redirected_to http://www.invisible.ch
```

Rendered with template

```
assert_template "post/index"
```

Variable assignments

```
assert_nil assigns(:some_variable)
assert_not_nil assigns(:some_variable)
assert_equal 17, assigns(:posts).size
```

Rendering of specific tags

```
Note: assert_tag is deprecated. Use assert_select instead.

Cheat sheet:
http://labnotes.org/svn/public/ruby/rails_plugins/assert_select/
      cheat/assert_select.html

assert_select "html:root>head>title", "Welcome"
assert_select "div#photo img[src=/path/to/train.png][alt=train]"
```

Integration Tests

```
rake test:integration
```

Hypothetical integration test:

```
require "#{File.dirname(__FILE__)}/../test_helper"

class UserManagementTest < ActionController::IntegrationTest
  fixtures :users, :preferences
  def test_register_new_user
    get "/login"
    assert_response :success
    assert_template "login/index"

    get "/register"
    assert_response :success
    assert_template "register/index"

    post "/register",
        :user_name => "happyjoe",
        :password => "neversad"
    assert_response :redirect
    follow_redirect!
    assert_response :success
    assert_template "welcome"
end
```

Learn more: *http://jamis.jamisbuck.org/articles/2006/03/09/integration-testing-in-rails-1-1*

More on Testing

Learn more: *http://manuals.rubyonrails.com/read/book/5*

rake

rake is the Ruby version of a **make** utility. Rails defines a number of rake tasks:

```
rake db:abort_if_pending_migrations   # Raises an error if there are pending...
rake db:charset                       # Retrieves the charset for the curren...
rake db:collation                     # Retrieves the collation for the curr...
rake db:create                        # Create the database defined in confi...
rake db:create:all                    # Create all the local databases defin...
rake db:drop                          # Drops the database for the current R...
rake db:drop:all                      # Drops all the local databases define...
rake db:fixtures:identify             # Search for a fixture given a LABEL o...
rake db:fixtures:load                 # Load fixtures into the current envir...
rake db:migrate                       # Migrate the database through scripts...
rake db:migrate:down                  # Runs the "down" for a given migratio...
rake db:migrate:redo                  # Rollbacks the database one migration...
rake db:migrate:reset                 # Resets your database using your migr...
rake db:migrate:up                    # Runs the "up" for a given migration ...
rake db:reset                         # Drops and recreates the database fro...
rake db:rollback                      # Rolls the schema back to the previou...
rake db:schema:dump                   # Create a db/schema.rb file that can ...
rake db:schema:load                   # Load a schema.rb file into the database
rake db:sessions:clear                # Clear the sessions table
rake db:sessions:create               # Creates a sessions migration for use...
rake db:structure:dump                # Dump the database structure to a SQL...
rake db:test:clone                    # Recreate the test database from the ...
rake db:test:clone_structure          # Recreate the test databases from the...
rake db:test:prepare                  # Prepare the test database and load t...
rake db:test:purge                    # Empty the test database
rake db:version                       # Retrieves the current schema version...
rake doc:app                          # Build the app HTML Files
rake doc:clobber_app                  # Remove rdoc products
rake doc:clobber_plugins              # Remove plugin documentation
rake doc:clobber_rails                # Remove rdoc products
rake doc:plugins                      # Generate documentation for all insta...
rake doc:rails                        # Build the rails HTML Files
rake doc:reapp                        # Force a rebuild of the RDOC files
rake doc:rerails                      # Force a rebuild of the RDOC files
rake gems                             # List the gems that this rails applic...
rake gems:build                       # Build any native extensions for unpa...
rake gems:install                     # Installs all required gems for this ...
rake gems:unpack                      # Unpacks the specified gem into vendo...
rake gems:unpack:dependencies         # Unpacks the specified gems and its d...
rake log:clear                        # Truncates all *.log files in log/ to...
rake notes                            # Enumerate all annotations
rake notes:fixme                      # Enumerate all FIXME annotations
rake notes:optimize                   # Enumerate all OPTIMIZE annotations
```

```
rake notes:todo                    # Enumerate all TODO annotations
rake rails:freeze:edge             # Lock to latest Edge Rails, for a spe...
rake rails:freeze:gems             # Lock this application to the current...
rake rails:unfreeze                # Unlock this application from freeze ...
rake rails:update                  # Update both configs, scripts and pub...
rake rails:update:configs          # Update config/boot.rb from your curr...
rake rails:update:javascripts      # Update your javascripts from your cu...
rake rails:update:scripts          # Add new scripts to the application s...
rake routes                        # Print out all defined routes in matc...
rake secret                        # Generate a crytographically secure s...
rake stats                         # Report code statistics (KLOCs, etc) ...
rake test                          # Run all unit, functional and integra...
rake test:functionals              # Run tests for functionalsdb:test:pre...
rake test:integration              # Run tests for integrationdb:test:pre...
rake test:plugins                  # Run tests for pluginsenvironment / R...
rake test:recent                   # Run tests for recentdb:test:prepare ...
rake test:uncommitted              # Run tests for uncommitteddb:test:pre...
rake test:units                    # Run tests for unitsdb:test:prepare /...
rake time:zones:all                # Displays names of all time zones rec...
rake time:zones:local              # Displays names of time zones recogni...
rake time:zones:us                 # Displays names of US time zones reco...
rake tmp:cache:clear               # Clears all files and directories in ...
rake tmp:clear                     # Clear session, cache, and socket fil...
rake tmp:create                    # Creates tmp directories for sessions...
rake tmp:pids:clear                # Clears all files in tmp/pids
rake tmp:sessions:clear            # Clears all files in tmp/sessions
rake tmp:sockets:clear             # Clears all files in tmp/sockets

rake --tasks                       # show all rake tasks
```

Generators

```
ruby script/generate model ModellName attribute1:type attribute2:type
ruby script/generate controller ListController show edit
ruby script/generate scaffold ModelName ControllerName attribute1:type attribute2:type
ruby script/generate migration AddNewTable
ruby script/generate resource ResourceName attribute1:type attribute2:type
ruby script/generate plugin PluginName
ruby script/generate mailer Notification lost_password signup
ruby script/generate web_service ServiceName api_one api_two
ruby script/generate integration_test TestName
ruby script/generate session_migration
ruby script/generate integration_test IntegrationTestName
ruby script/generate observer ModelName
```

Options:

-p *or* --pretend

Run but do not make any changes.

-f *or* --force

Overwrite files that already exist.

-s *or* --skip

Skip files that already exist.

-q *or* --quiet
:   Suppress normal output.

-t *or* --backtrace
:   Debugging: show backtrace on errors.

-h *or* --help
:   Show this help message.

-c *or* --svn
:   Modify files with subversion (note: svn must be in path).

Plug-ins

```
Install a plugin:
  plugin install continuous_builder

Install a plugin from a subversion URL:
  plugin install http://dev.rubyonrails.com/svn/rails/plugins/continu...

Install a plugin from a git URL:
  plugin install git://github.com/SomeGuy/my_awesome_plugin.git

Install a plugin and add a svn:externals entry to vendor/plugins
  plugin install -x continuous_builder

List all available plugins:
  plugin list

List plugins in the specified repository:
  plugin list --source=http://dev.rubyonrails.com/svn/rails/plugins/

Discover and prompt to add new repositories:
  plugin discover

Discover new repositories but just list them, don't add anything:
  plugin discover -l

Add a new repository to the source list:
  plugin source http://dev.rubyonrails.com/svn/rails/plugins/

Remove a repository from the source list:
  plugin unsource http://dev.rubyonrails.com/svn/rails/plugins/

Show currently configured repositories:
  plugin sources
```

Learn more: *http://wiki.rubyonrails.com/rails/pages/Plugins*

Searchable directory of plug-ins: *http://www.agilewebdevelopment.com/plugins*

RJS (Ruby JavaScript)

This example:

```
update_page do |page|
  page.insert_html :bottom, 'list', "<li>#{@item.name}</li>"
  page.visual_effect :highlight, 'list'
  page.hide 'status-indicator', 'cancel-link'
end
```

generates the following JavaScript:

```
new Insertion.Bottom("list", "<li>Some item</li>");
new Effect.Highlight("list");
["status-indicator", "cancel-link"].each(Element.hide);
```

Learn more:

- *http://api.rubyonrails.com/classes/ActionView/Helpers/PrototypeHelper/JavaScript Generator/GeneratorMethods.html*
- *http://www.codyfauser.com/articles/2005/11/20/rails-rjs-templates*
- *http://scottraymond.net/articles/2005/12/01/real-world-rails-rjs-templates*
- *http://www.rubynoob.com/articles/2006/05/13/simple-rails-rjs-tutorial*

Active Record

Automated Mapping

Automatically maps:

- Tables → classes
- Rows → objects (instances of model classes)
- Columns → object attributes

Table to class mapping uses English plurals:

- An `Invoice` model class maps to an `invoices` table.
- A `Person` model class maps to a `people` table.
- A `Country` model class maps to a `countries` table.
- A `SecurityLevel` model class maps to a `security_levels` table.

Learn more: *http://api.rubyonrails.com/classes/ActiveRecord/Base.html*

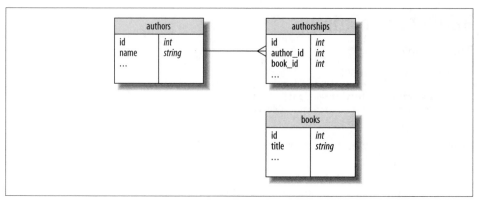

Figure B-1. One-to-one and one-to-many relationships

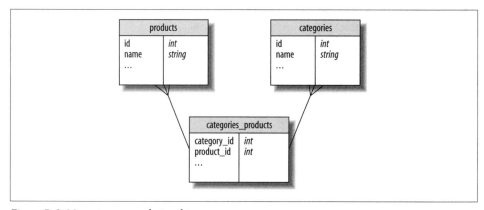

Figure B-2. Many-to-many relationships

Associations

Four ways of associating models (see also Figures B-1 and B-2):

```
has_one
has_many
belongs_to
has_and_belongs_to_many
def Order < ActiveRecord::Base
  has_many :line_items
  belongs_to :customer    # there's a column "customer_id" in the db table
end

def LineItem < ActiveRecord::Base
  belongs_to :order # there's a column "order_id" in the db table
end

def Customer < ActiveRecord::Base
  has_many :orders
  has_one :address, :as => addressable
```

```
end

def Address < ActiveRecord::Base
  belongs_to :addressable, :polymorphic => true
end

belongs_to  :some_model,
        :class_name  => 'MyClass',     # specifies other class name
        :foreign_key => 'my_real_id',  # and primary key
        :conditions  => 'column = 0'   # only finds when this condition met
        :polymporphic => boolean       # true if more than one target type

has_one :some_model,
        # as belongs_to and additionally:
        :dependent  => :destroy        # deletes associated object
        :order      => 'name ASC'      # SQL fragment for sorting

has_many :some_model
        # as has_one and additionally:
        :dependent => :destroy         # deletes all dependent data
                                       # calling each objects destroy
        :dependent => :delete_all      # deletes all dependent data
                                       # without calling the destroy methods
        :dependent => :nullify         # set association to null, not
                                       # destroying objects
        :group => 'name'               # adds GROUP BY fragment
        :finder_sql => 'select ....'   # instead of the Rails finders
        :counter_sql => 'select ...'   # instead of the Rails counters
        :as => 'polymorph interface'   # the target is polymorphic

def Category < ActiveRecord::Base
  has_and_belongs_to_many :products
end

def Product < ActiveRecord::Base
  has_and_belongs_to_many :categories
end
```

Table addresses:

- Has addressable_id column
- Has addressable_type column containing the id of the target association

Table categories_products:

- Has category_id column
- Has product_id column
- Does not have id column

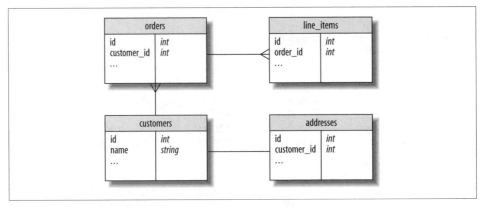

Figure B-3. Through model

Association Join Models (As Shown in Figure B-3)

```
class Author < ActiveRecord::Base
  has_many :authorships
  has_many :books, :through => :authorships
end

class Authorship < ActiveRecord::Base
  belongs_to :author
  belongs_to :book
end

class Book < ActiveRecord::Base
  has_one :authorship
end

@author = Author.find :first
@author.authorships.collect { |a| a.book } # selects all books that the author's
                                           # authorships belong to.
@author.books                              # selects all books by using the Authorship
                                           # join model
```

Also works through has_many associations:

```
class Firm < ActiveRecord::Base
  has_many    :clients
  has_many    :invoices, :through => :clients
  has_many    :paid_invoices, :through => :clients, :source => :invoice
end

class Client < ActiveRecord::Base
  belongs_to :firm
  has_many    :invoices
end

class Invoice < ActiveRecord::Base
  belongs_to :client
end
```

```
@firm = Firm.find :first
@firm.clients.collect { |c| c.invoices }.flatten  # select all invoices for all clients
                                                  # of the firm
@firm.invoices                                    # selects all invoices by going
                                                  # through the Client join model.
```

Learn more at the following address: *http://api.rubyonrails.com/classes/ActiveRecord/ Associations/ClassMethods.html*

Validations

```
validates_presence_of :firstname, :lastname     # must be filled out

validates_length_of :password,
                    :minimum => 8           # more than 8 characters
                    :maximum => 16          # shorter than 16 characters
                    :in => 8..16            # between 8 and 16 characters
                    :too_short => 'way too short'
                    :too_long => 'way too long'

validates_acceptance_of :eula           # Must accept a condition
                    :accept => 'Y'      # default: 1 (ideal for a checkbox)

validates_confirmation_of :password
# the fields password and password_confirmation must match

validates_uniqueness_of :user_name              # user_name has to be unique
                    :scope => 'account_id'  # Condition:
                                            # account_id = user.account_id

validates_format_of :email          # field must match a regular expression
                    :with => /^(+)@((?:[-a-z0-9]+/.)+[a-z]{2,})$/i

validates_numericality_of   :value          # value is numeric
                    :only_integer => true
                    :allow_nil => true

validates_inclusion_in  :gender,    # value is in enumeration
                    :in => %w( m, f )

validates_exclusion_of  :age        # value is not in Enumeration
                    :in => 13..19   # don't want any teenagers

validates_associated :relation
# validates that the associated object is valid
```

Validation options:

```
:message => 'my own errormessage'
:on      => :create         # or :update (validates only then)
:if      => ...             # call method oder Proc
```

Learn more: *http://api.rubyonrails.com/classes/ActiveRecord/Validations.html*

Calculations

```
Person.average :age
Person.minimum :age
Person.maximum :age
Person.count
Person.count(:conditions => "age > 26")
Person.sum :salary, :group => :last_name
```

Learn more at the following address: *http://api.rubyonrails.com/classes/ActiveRecord/Calculations/ClassMethods.html*

Finders

```
find(42)                                       # object with ID 42
find([37, 42])                                 # Array with the objects with id 37, 42
find :all
find :first,
     :conditions => [ "name = ?", "Hans" ]     # finds the first record
                                               # with matching condition
```

More parameters for `find`:

```
:order => 'name DESC'              # sql fragment for sorting
:offset => 20                      # starts with entry 20
:limit => 10                       # only return 10 objects
:group => 'name'                   # sql fragment GROUP BY
:joins => 'LEFT JOIN ...'          # additional LEFT JOIN (rarely used)
:include => [:account, :friends]   # LEFT OUTER JOIN with these models
:include => { :groups => { :members=> { :favorites } } }
:select => [:name, :adress]        # instead of SELECT * FROM
:readonly => true                  # objects are write protected
```

Dynamic attribute-based finders

```
Person.find_by_user_name(user_name)
Person.find_all_by_last_name(last_name)
Person.find_by_user_name_and_password(user_name, password)
Order.find_by_name("Joe Blow")
Order.find_by_email("jb@gmail.com")
Slideshow.find_or_create_by_name("Winter")
```

Learn more: *http://api.rubyonrails.com/classes/ActiveRecord/Base.html*

Scope

```
Employee.with_scope(
    :find => { :conditions => "salary > 10000",
               :limit => 10 }) do
  Employee.find(:all)     # => SELECT * FROM employees
                          #             WHERE (salary > 10000)
                          #             LIMIT 10

  # scope is cumulative
  Employee.with_scope(
```

```
                :find => { :conditions => "name = 'Jamis'" }) do
        Employee.find(:all)   # => SELECT * FROM employees
                              #              WHERE ( salary > 10000 )
                              #              AND ( name = 'Jamis' ))
                              #              LIMIT 10
      end

      # all previous scope is ignored
      Employee.with_exclusive_scope(
        :find => { :conditions => "name = 'Jamis'" }) do
        Employee.find(:all)   # => SELECT * FROM employees
                              #              WHERE (name = 'Jamis')
      end
    end
```

Learn more:

- *http://www.codyfauser.com/articles/2006/02/01/using-with_scope-to-refactor
  -messy-finders*
- *http://blog.caboo.se/articles/2006/02/22/nested-with_scope*

Named scope

```
    class Employee
      named_scope :active, :conditions => 'end_date = null'

      named_scope :with_salary, lambda {|s| { :conditions => ["salary > ?", s]} }
    end

    # All of the following are possible
    employee.active
    employee.with_salary(10000)
    employee.active.with_salary(10000)
```

Learn more:

- *http://www.codyfauser.com/articles/2006/02/01/using-with_scope-to-refactor
  -messy-finders*
- *http://blog.caboo.se/articles/2006/02/22/nested-with_scope*
- *http://pivots.pivotallabs.com/users/nick/blog/articles/284-hasfinder-it-s-now-easier
  -than-ever-to-create-complex-re-usable-sql-queries*
- *http://railscasts.com/episodes/108*

Acts

acts_as_list:

```
                script/plugin install acts_as_list

                class TodoList < ActiveRecord::Base
      has_many :todo_items, :order => "position"
    end
```

```
class TodoItem < ActiveRecord::Base
  belongs_to :todo_list
  acts_as_list :scope => :todo_list
end

todo_list.first.move_to_bottom
todo_list.last.move_higher
```

Learn more:

- *http://api.rubyonrails.com/classes/ActiveRecord/Acts/List/ClassMethods.html*
- *http://api.rubyonrails.com/classes/ActiveRecord/Acts/List/InstanceMethods.html*

acts_as_tree:

```
              script/plugin install acts_as_tree
              class Category < ActiveRecord::Base
  acts_as_tree :order => "name"
end

Example :
root
 /_ child1
      /_ subchild1
      /_ subchild2

root     = Category.create("name" => "root")
child1   = root.children.create("name" => "child1")
subchild1 = child1.children.create("name" => "subchild1")

root.parent   # => nil
child1.parent # => root
root.children # => [child1]
root.children.first.children.first # => subchild1
```

Learn more here: *http://api.rubyonrails.com/classes/ActiveRecord/Acts/Tree/ClassMe thods.html*

Callbacks

Callbacks are hooks into the life cycle of an Active Record object that allows you to trigger logic before or after an alteration of the object state (see Table B-1).

Table B-1. Active Record object life cycle

Object state	Callback
save	
valid?	
	before_validation
	before_validation_on_create

Object state	Callback
validate	
validate_on_create	
	after_validation
	after_validation_on_create
	before_save
	before_create
create	
	after_create
	after_save

Example:

```
class Subscription < ActiveRecord::Base
  before_create :record_signup
private
  def record_signup
    self.signed_up_on = Date.today
  end
end

class Firm < ActiveRecord::Base
  # Destroys the associated clients and people when the firm is destroyed
  before_destroy { |record| Person.destroy_all "firm_id = #{record.id}"   }
  before_destroy { |record| Client.destroy_all "client_of = #{record.id}" }
end
```

Learn more: *http://api.rubyonrails.com/classes/ActiveRecord/Callbacks.html*

Observers

The Observer classes let you extract the functionality of the callbacks:

```
class CommentObserver < ActiveRecord::Observer
  def after_save(comment)
    Notifications.deliver_comment("admin@do.com", "New comment was posted", comment)
  end
end
```

- Store observers in *app/model/model_observer.rb.*
- Enable observer by putting this in *config/environment.rb:*

```
config.active_record.observers = :comment_observer, :signup_observer
```

Learn more: *http://api.rubyonrails.com/classes/ActiveRecord/Observer.html*

Migration

```
>ruby script/generate migration MyAddTables
```

Creates the file *db/migrations/23495834677_my_add_tables.rb*. The methods up() and
down() change the db schema:

```
def self.up      # brings db schema to the next version
  create_table :table, :force => true do |t|
    t.column :name, :string
    t.column :age, :integer, { :default => 42 }
    t.column :description, :text
    # :string, :text, :integer, :float, :datetime, :timestamp, :time, :date,
    # :binary, :boolean
  end
  add_column :table, :column, :type
  rename_column :table, :old_name, :new_name
  change_column :table, :column, :new_type
  execute "SQL Statement"
  add_index :table, :column, :unique => true, :name => 'some_name'
  add_index :table, [ :column1, :column2 ]
end

def self.down    # rollbacks changes
  rename_column :table, :new_name, :old_name
  remove_column :table, :column
  drop_table :table
  remove_index :table, :column
end
```

To execute the migration:

```
> rake db:migrate
> rake db:migrate:up
> rake db:migrate:down
> rake db:migrate VERSION=23495834677
> rake db:migrate RAILS_ENV=production
```

Learn more: *http://api.rubyonrails.org/classes/ActiveRecord/Migration.html*

Controllers

REST

Rails uses REST conventions to access resources. REST is a way of organizing HTTP
requests. This is the mapping between a REST-style HTTP command, the corresponding Rails controller action, and the corresponding database command, as shown in
Table B-2.

Table B-2. REST

	Create	Read	Update	Delete
HTTP	POST	GET	PUT	DELETE
RAILS	CREATE	SHOW	UPDATE	DESTROY
Database	INSERT	SELECT	UPDATE	DELETE

These are the specific HTTP requests that will invoke these controller methods if the map `resource :slide` statement appears in *routes.rb*:

```
class SlidesController < ApplicationController
  # GET /slides
  # GET /slides.xml
  def index
    ...
  end

  # GET /slides/1
  # GET /slides/1.xml
  def show
    ...
  end

  # GET /slides/new
  # GET /slides/new.xml
  def new
    ...
  end

  # GET /slides/1/edit
  def edit
    ...
  end

  # POST /slides
  # POST /slides.xml
  def create
    ...
  end

  # PUT /slides/1
  # PUT /slides/1.xml
  def update
    ...
  end

  # DELETE /slides/1
  # DELETE /slides/1.xml
  def destroy
    ...
  end
end
```

Named routes

Mapping a resource in *config/routes.rb* will generate some named routes and some helpers:

```
map.resource :photo

  Named Route   Helpers
  ============  =============================================
  photo         account_url, hash_for_account_url,
                account_path, hash_for_account_path

  new_photo     new_account_url, hash_for_new_account_url,
                new_account_path, hash_for_new_account_path

  edit_photo    edit_account_url, hash_for_edit_account_url,
                edit_account_path, hash_for_edit_account_path


examples
========
link_to "Show a photo", photo
link_to "Edit a photo", edit_photo_path(photo)
link_to "Create a photo", new_photo_path

redirect_to photos_url
redirect_to @photo
```

Controller Methods

Each public method in a controller is callable by the default URL scheme */controller/ action* (/world/hello, in this example):

```
class WorldController < ApplicationController
def hello
  render :text => 'Hello world'
end
```

All request parameters, whether they come from a GET or POST request, or from the URL, are available through the **params** hash:

```
/world/hello/1?foo=bar
id = params[:id]     # 1
foo = params[:foo]   # bar
```

Instance variables defined in the controller's methods are available to the corresponding view templates:

```
def show
  @person = Person.find( params[:id])
end
```

Determine the type of response accepted:

```
def index
  @posts = Post.find :all
```

```
  respond_to do |type|
    type.html # using defaults, which will render weblog/index.html.erb
    type.xml  { render :action => "index.xml.erb" }
    type.js   { render :action => "index.rjs" }
  end
end
```

Learn more: *http://api.rubyonrails.com/classes/ActionController/Base.html*

Render

Generally, the view template with the same name as the controller method is used to render the results.

Action

```
render :action => 'some_action'    # the default. Does not need to be specified
                                   # in a controller method called "some_action"
render :action => 'another_action', :layout => false
render :action => 'some_action', :layout => 'another_layout'
```

Partials

Partials are stored in files whose filename begins with an underscore (such as _error, _subform, and _listitem):

```
render :partial => 'subform'
render :partial => 'error', :status => 500
render :partial => 'subform', :locals => { :variable => @other_variable }
render :partial => 'listitem', :collection => @list
render :partial => 'listitem', :collection => @list, :spacer_template =>
'list_divider'
```

Templates

Similar to rendering an action, but finds the template based on the template root (*app/ views*):

```
render :template => 'weblog/show'  # renders app/views/weblog/show
```

Files

```
render :file => '/path/to/some/file.html.erb'
render :file => '/path/to/some/filenotfound.html.erb', status => 404, :layout => true
```

Text

```
render :text => "Hello World"
render :text => "This is an error", :status => 500
```

```
render :text => "Let's use a layout", :layout => true
render :text => 'Specific layout', :layout => 'special'
```

Inline Template

Uses render :inline to render the "miniature" template:

```
render :inline => "<%= 'hello, ' * 3 + 'again' %>"
render :inline => "<%= 'hello ' + name %>", :locals => { :name => "david" }
```

RJS

```
def refresh
  render :update do |page|
    page.replace_html 'user_list', :partial => 'user', :collection => @users
    page.visual_effect :highlight, 'user_list'
  end
end
```

Change content_type

```
render :action => "atom.xml.erb", :content_type => "application/atom+xml"
```

Redirects

```
redirect_to(:action => "edit")
redirect_to(:controller => "accounts", :action => "signup")
redirect_to(@account)
redirect_to(edit_path(@photo))
```

Nothing

```
render :nothing
render :nothing, :status => 403    # forbidden
```

Learn more:

- *http://api.rubyonrails.com/classes/ActionView/Base.html*
- *http://api.rubyonrails.com/classes/ActionController/Base.html*

URL Routing

In *config/routes.rb*:

```
map.connect '', :controller => 'posts', :action => 'list' # default
map.connect ':action/:controller/:id'
map.connect 'tasks/:year/:month', :controller => 'tasks',
                                  :action => 'by_date',
                                  :month => nil, :year => nil,
                                  :requirements => {:year => //d{4}/,
                                                    :month => //d{1,2}/ }
```

```
map.resource :account

map.resources :orders do |line_item|
  order.resource :line_item
end
```

Learn more: *http://manuals.rubyonrails.com/read/chapter/65*

Filter

Filters can change a request before or after the controller. They can, for example, be used for authentication, encryption, or compression:

```
before_filter :login_required, :except => [ :login ]
before_filter :autenticate, :only => [ :edit, :delete ]
after_filter :compress
```

It's also possible to use a **proc** for a really small filter action:

```
before_filter { |controller| false if controller.params["stop_action"] }
```

Change the order of your filters with `prepend_before_filter` and `prepend_after_filter` (like `prepend_before_filter :some_filter`, which will put the `some_filter` at the beginning of the filter chain).

If you define a filter in a superclass, you can skip it in the subclass:

```
skip_before_filter :some_filter
skip_after_filter :some_filter
```

Learn more: *http://api.rubyonrails.com/classes/ActionController/Filters/ClassMethods .html*

Session/Flash

To save data across multiple requests, you can use either the session or the flash hashes. A flash stores a value (normally text) until the next request, while a session stores data during the complete session:

```
session[:user] = @user
flash[:message] = "Data was saved successfully"

<%= link_to "login", :action => 'login' unless session[:user] %>
<% if flash[:message] %>
<div><%= h flash[:message] %></div>
<% end %>
```

Session management

It's possible to turn off session management:

```
session :off                     # turn session managment off
session :off, :only => :action   # only for this :action
```

```
session :off, :except => :action    # except for this action
session :only => :foo,               # only for :foo when doing HTTPS
        :session_secure => true
session :off, :only => :foo,         # off for foo, if uses as Web Service
        :if => Proc.new { |req| req.parameters[:ws] }
```

Learn more at the following site: *http://api.rubyonrails.com/classes/ActionController/SessionManagement/ClassMethods.html*

Cookies

Setting

```
cookies[:user_name] = "david" # => Will set a simple session cookie
cookies[:login] = { :value => "XJ-122", :expires => Time.now + 3600}
    # => Will set a cookie that expires in 1 hour
```

Reading

```
cookies[:user_name] # => "david"
cookies.size         # => 2
```

Deleting

```
cookies.delete :user_name
```

Option symbols for setting cookies:

value
> The cookie's value or list of values (as an array).

path
> The path for which this cookie applies (defaults to the root of the application).

domain
> The domain for which this cookie applies.

expires
> The time at which this cookie expires, as a Time object.

secure
> Whether this cookie is secure (defaults to false). Secure cookies are transmitted only to HTTPS servers.

Learn more: *http://api.rubyonrails.com/classes/ActionController/Cookies.html*

Views

View Templates

All view templates are stored in *app/views/controllername*. The extension determines what kind of template it is:

*.html.erb
>   Ruby HTML (using *wish.name_and_quantity*)

*.xml.erb
>   Ruby XML (using Builder)

*.rjs
>   Ruby JavaScript

All instance variables of the controller are available to the view. In addition, the following special objects can be accessed:

headers
>   The headers of the outgoing response

request
>   The incoming request object

response
>   The outgoing response object

params
>   The parameter hash

session
>   The session hash

controller
>   The current controller

html.erb

html.erb is HTML mixed with Ruby, by using tags. All of Ruby is available for programming:

```
<% %>   # executes the Ruby code
<%= %>  # executes the Ruby code and displays the result

<ul>
<% @products.each do |p| %>
  <li><%= h @p.name %></li>
<% end %>
</ul>
```

The output of anything in <%= %> tags is directly copied to the HTML output stream. To secure against HTML injection, use the h() function to HTML-escape the output. For example:

```
<%=h @user_entered_notes %>
```

xml.erb

Creates XML files:

```
xml.instruct!                  # <?xml version="1.0" encoding="UTF-8"?>
xml.comment! "a comment"       # <!-- a comment -->
xml.feed "xmlns" => "http://www.w3.org/2005/Atom" do
  xml.title "My Atom Feed"
  xml.subtitle h(@feed.subtitle), "type" => 'html'
  xml.link url_for( :only_path => false,
                    :controller => 'feed',
                    :action => 'atom' )
  xml.updated @updated.iso8601
  xml.author do
    xml.name "Jens-Christian Fischer"
    xml.email "jcfischer@gmail.com"
  end
  @entries.each do |entry|
    xml.entry do
      xml.title entry.title
      xml.link "href" => url_for ( :only_path => false,
                                   :controller => 'entries',
                                   :action => 'show',
                                   :id => entry )
      xml.id entry.urn
      xml.updated entry.updated.iso8601
      xml.summary h(entry.summary)
    end
  end
end
```

Learn more: *http://rubyforge.org/projects/builder/*

RJS

In addition to HTML and XML templates, Rails also understands JavaScript templates. They allow you to easily create complex alterations of the displayed page. You can manipulate a page element with the following methods:

select

Select a DOM element for further processing:

```
page.select('pattern') # selects an item on the page through a CSS pattern
                       # select('p'), select('p.welcome b')
page.select('div.header em').first.hide
page.select('#items li').eacj do |value|
```

```
        value.hide
      end
```

`insert_html`

>   Inserts content into the DOM at a specific position:

```
      page.insert_html :position, id, content
```

>   `position` can be one of the following:

```
      :top
      :bottom
      :before
      :after
```

`replace_html`

>   Replaces the inner HTML of the specified DOM element:

```
      page.replace_html 'title', "This is the new title"
      page.replace_html 'person-45', :partial => 'person', :object => @person
```

`replace`

>   Replaces the outer HTML (i.e., the entire element) of the specified DOM element:

```
      page.replace 'task', :partial => 'task', :object => @task
```

`remove`

>   Removes the specified DOM element:

```
      page.remove 'edit-button'
```

`hide`

>   Hides the specified DOM element:

```
      page.hide 'some-element'
```

`show`

>   Shows the specified DOM element:

```
      page.show 'some-element'
```

`toggle`

>   Toggles the visibility of a DOM element:

```
      page.toggle 'some-element'
```

`alert`

>   Displays an alert box:

```
      page.alert 'Hello world'
```

`redirect_to`

>   Redirects the browser to a given location:

```
      page.redirect_to :controller => 'blog', :action => 'show', :id => @post
```

`call`
>   Calls another JavaScript function:
>
>    ```
>    page.call foo, 1, 2
>    ```

`assign`
>   Assigns a value to a JavaScript variable:
>
>    ```
>    page.assign "foo", 42
>    ```

`<<`
>   Writes raw JavaScript to the page:
>
>    ```
>    page << "alert('hello world');"
>    ```

`delay`
>   Delays the code in the block by a number of seconds:
>
>    ```
>    page.delay(10) do
>        page.visual_effect :fade, 'notice'
>    end
>    ```

`visual_effect`
>   Calls a Scriptaculous effect:
>
>    ```
>    page.visual_effect :highlight, 'notice', :duration => 2
>    ```

`sortable`
>   Creates a sortable element:
>
>    ```
>    page.sortable 'my_list', :url => { :action => 'order' }
>    ```

`dragable`
>   Creates a draggable element:
>
>    ```
>    page.dragable 'my_image', :revert => true
>    ```

`drop_receiving`
>   Creates an element for receiving drops:
>
>    ```
>    page.drop_recieving 'my_cart', :url => { :controller => 'cart',
>                                             :action => 'add' }
>    ```

Learn more: *http://api.rubyonrails.com/classes/ActionView/Base.html*

Helpers

Small functions, normally used for displaying data, can be extracted to helpers. Each view has its own helper class (in *app/helpers*). Common functionality is stored in *app/helpers/application_helper.rb*.

Links

```
link_to "Name", :controller => 'post', :action => 'show', :id => @post.id
link_to "Delete", { :controller => "admin",
  :action => "delete",
  :id => @post },
{ :class => 'css-class',
  :id => 'css-id',
  :confirm => "Are you sure?" }

image_tag "spinner.png", :class => "image", :alt => "Spinner"

mail_to "info@invisible.ch", "send mail",
    :subject => "Support request by #{@user.name}",
    :cc => @user.email,
    :body => '....',
    :encoding => "javascript"

stylesheet_link_tag "scaffold", "admin", :media => "all"
```

Learn more: *http://api.rubyonrails.com/classes/ActionView/Helpers/UrlHelper.html*

HTML Forms

Form

```
<%= form_tag { :action => :save }, { :method => :post } %>
```

This creates a form tag with the specified action, and makes it a POST request.

Use :multipart => true to define a MIME-multipart form (for file uploads).

Text fields

```
<%= text_field :modelname, :attribute_name, options %>
```

The following creates a text input field of the form:

```
<input type="text" name="modelname[attribute_name]" id="attributename" />
```

Example:

```
text_field "post", "title", "size" => 20
    <input   type="text" id="post_title" name="post[title]"
             size="20" value="#{@post.title}" />
```

Create a hidden field:

```
<%= hidden_field ... %>
```

Create a password field (all input shown as stars):

```
<%= password_field ... %>
```

Create a file field:

```
<%= file_field ... %>
```

Text area

```
<%= text_area ... %>
```

This example:

```
text_area "post", "body", "cols" => 20, "rows" => 40
```

generates:

```
<textarea cols="20" rows="40" id="post_body" name="post[body]">
    #{@post.body}
</textarea>
```

Radio button

```
<%= radio_button :modelname, :attribute, :tag_value, options %>
```

Example:

```
radio_button "post", "category", "rails"
radio_button "post", "category", "java"
    <input type="radio" id="post_category" name="post[category]" value="rails"
        checked="checked" />
    <input type="radio" id="post_category" name="post[category]" value="java" />
```

Checkbox

```
<%= check_box :modelname, :attribute, options, on_value, off_value %>
```

Example:

```
check_box "post", "validated"    # post.validated? returns 1 or 0
    <input type="checkbox" id="post_validate" name="post[validated]"
        value="1" checked="checked" />
    <input name="post[validated]" type="hidden" value="0" />

check_box "puppy", "gooddog", {}, "yes", "no"
    <input type="checkbox" id="puppy_gooddog" name="puppy[gooddog]" value="yes" />
    <input name="puppy[gooddog]" type="hidden" value="no" />
```

Options

Creates a select tag. Pass an array of choices:

```
<%= select :variable, :attribute, choices, options,

html_options %>
```

Example:

```
select  "post",
        "person_id",
        Person.find_all.collect {|p| [ p.name, p.id ] },
        { :include_blank => true }

  <select name="post[person_id]">
    <option></option>
```

```
      <option value="1" selected="selected">David</option>
      <option value="2">Sam</option>
      <option value="3">Tobias</option>
    </select>

    <%= collection_select :variable, :attribute, choices, :id, :value %>
```

Date and time

```
<%= date_select :variable, :attribute, options %>
<%= datetime_select :variable, :attribute, options %>
```

Examples:

```
date_select "post", "written_on"
date_select "user", "birthday", :start_year => 1910
date_select "user", "cc_date", :start_year => 2005,
                               :use_month_numbers => true,
                               :discard_day => true,
                               :order => [:year, :month]

datetime_select "post", "written_on"
```

end_form tag

```
<%= end_form_tag %>
```

Learn more: *http://api.rubyonrails.com/classes/ActionView/Helpers/FormHelper.html*

Layouts

A layout defines the surroundings of an HTML page. You use it to define a common
look and feel. Layouts live in *app/views/layouts*:

```
<html>
  <head>
    <title>Form: <%= controller.action_name %></title>
    <%= stylesheet_link_tag 'scaffold' %>
  </head>
  <body>
    <%= yield %>    # the content will show up here
  </body>
</html>
----
class MyController < ApplicationController
  layout "standard", :except => [ :rss, :atom ]
...
end
----
class MyOtherController < ApplicationController
  layout :compute_layout

  # this method computes the name of the layout to use
  def compute_layout
    return "admin" if session[:role] == "admin"
```

```
        "standard"
    end
    ...
end
```

Layouts have access to the instance variables of the controller.

Learn more: *http://api.rubyonrails.com/classes/ActionController/Layout/ClassMethods .html*

Partials

Partials are building blocks for creating views. They allow you to reuse commonly used display blocks. They are stored in files:

```
render :partial => 'product'
```

This command loads the partial in *_product.rthml* and passes the instance variable @product to it. The partial can access it using **@product**:

```
render :partial => 'product', :locals => { :product => @bought }
```

This command loads the same partial, but assigns a different instance variable to it:

```
render :partial => 'product', :collection => @product_list
```

This renders the partial for each element in **@product_list** and assigns **@product** to each element. An iteration counter is automatically made available to the template with a name of the form **partial_name_counter** (in the previous example, **product_counter**).

Learn more: *http://api.rubyonrails.com/classes/ActionView/Partials.html*

Ajax

Be sure to include the JavaScript libraries in the layout:

```
<%= javascript_include_tag :defaults %>
```

Linking to Remote Action

```
<%= link_to_remote "link", :update => 'some_div',
                           :url => { :action => 'show', :id => post.id } %>

<%= link_to_remote "link", :url => { :action => 'create',
                           :update => { :success => 'good_div',
                                              :failure => 'error_div' },
                           :loading => 'Element.show('spinner'),
                           :complete => 'Element.hide('spinner') } %>
```

Callbacks

`:loading`
> Called when the remote document is being loaded with data by the browser.

`:loaded`
> Called when the browser has finished loading the remote document.

`:interactive`
> Called when the user can interact with the remote document, even though it has not finished loading.

`:success`
> Called when the XMLHttpRequest is completed, and the HTTP status code is in the 2XX range.

`:failure`
> Called when the XMLHttpRequest is completed, and the HTTP status code is not in the 2XX range.

`:complete`
> Called when the XMLHttpRequest is complete (fires after success/failure if they are present).

You can also specify reactions to return codes directly:

```
link_to_remote word,
    :url => { :action => "action" },
    404 => "alert('Not found...? Wrong URL...?')",
    :failure => "alert('HTTP Error ' + request.status + '!')"
```

Ajax Forms

You can create a form that will submit via an XMLHttpRequest instead of a POST request. The parameters are passed exactly the same way (so the controller can use the `params` method to access the parameters). Fallback for non-JavaScript-enabled browsers can be specified by using the `:action` methods in the `:html` option:

```
form_remote_tag :html => { :action => url_for(:controller => 'controller',
                                              :action => 'action'),
                           :method => :post }
```

Autocompleting Text Field

In the view template:

```
<%= text_field_with_auto_complete :model, :attribute %>
```

In the controller:

```
auto_complete_for :model, :attribute
```

Observe Field

```
<label for="search">Search term:</label>
<%= text_field_tag :search %>
<%= observe_field(:search,
                   :frequency => 0.5,
                   :update => :results,
                   :url => { :action => :search }) %>
<div id="results"></div>
```

Optionally, specify:

```
:on => :blur    # trigger for event (default :changed or :clicked)
:with => ...    # a JavaScript expression to specify what value is sent
                # defaults to "value"
:with => 'bla'  # "'bla' = value"
:with => 'a=b'  # "a=b"
```

Observe Form

Same semantics as observe_field.

periodically_call_remote

```
<%= periodically_call_remote(:update => 'process-list',
                              :url => { :action => :ps },
                              :frequency => 2 ) %>
```

Learn more: *http://api.rubyonrails.com/classes/ActionView/Helpers/JavaScriptHelper*
.html

Configuring Your Application

A lot of things can be configured in the *config/environment.rb* file. This list is not exhaustive.

Session Configuration

```
config.action_controller.session_store = :active_record_store
# one of :active_record_store, :drb_store,
# :mem_cache_store, or :memory_store or your own class

ActionController::Base.session_options[:session_key] = 'my_app'
    # use an application specific session_key
ActionController::Base.session_options[:session_id] = '12345'
    # use this session_id. Will be created if not specified
ActionController::Base.session_options[:session_expires] = 3.minute.from_now
    # how long before a session expires?
ActionController::Base.session_options[:new_session] = true
    # force the creation of a new session
ActionController::Base.session_options[:session_secure] = true
```

```
    # only use sessions over HTTPS
ActionController::Base.session_options[:session_domain] = 'invisible.ch'
    # Specify which domain this session is valid for (default: hostname of server)
ActionController::Base.session_options[:session_path] = '/my_app'
    # the path for which this session applies.  Defaults to the
    # directory of the CGI script
```

Learn more: *http://api.rubyonrails.com/classes/ActionController/SessionManagement/ClassMethods.html*

Caching Configuration

```
ActionController::Base.fragment_cache_store = :file_store, "/path/to/cache/directory"
```

Learn more: *http://api.rubyonrails.com/classes/ActionController/Caching.html*

Index

Symbols

" (double quotes)
    delimiting strings, 81
' (single quotes)
    delimiting strings, 81
() (parentheses)
    in Ruby, 82
:through relationship, 69
<associations>.clear method, 64
_ (underscore)
    in names, 43

A

accessor method, 45, 46
Action Pack
    building views, 12
actions
    controller, 179
    linking to remote, 190
Active Records, 37–58, 167–176
    about, 37
    acts, 173
    association join models, 170
    attributes, 44–47
    calculations, 172
    callbacks, 174
    classes, 42, 47–52
    CRUD operations, 52–57
    finders, 52, 172
    generating models, 39–42
    migration, 176
    observers, 175
    relationships, 59–76, 168
    validation, 171

acts
    Active Records, 173
acts_as_list relationship, 69
acts_as_nested_set macro, 75
acts_as_tree relationship, 69
Ajax (asynchronous JavaScript and XML), 103–121
    drag-and-drop, 106–118
    filtering by category, 118
    Rails implementation of, 103
    slideshow example, 104
    summary, 190–192
Ajax forms, 191
Apache web server, 7
app directory, 4
application.rb file, 9
applications
    configuring, 192
    creating, 161
assertions
    defined, 125
    in Rails, 147
    in Ruby, 125
    testing, 147
assert_difference assertion, 132
assert_difference method, 138
assert_nothing_raised assertion, 133
<association> attribute, 62
association join models, 170
<association>.nil? method, 61
associations, 59–76
    belongs_to, 60
    between resources, 18
    has_many, 62–65
    has_one, 65–75

We'd like to hear your suggestions for improving our indexes. Send email to *index@oreilly.com*.

About the Authors

Bruce A. Tate is a kayaker, mountain biker, and father of two. In his spare time, he is the CTO of WellGood, LLC, in Austin. WellGood is a team of social entrepreneurs who try to find sustainable revenue models for solving social problems such as reducing poverty and improving education. Bruce is also an international speaker and teacher. The 12-time author's books include *From Java to Ruby* and *Deploying Rails Applications* (both from Pragmatic Bookshelf), and *Beyond Java* (O'Reilly). Before WellGood, Bruce was an independent consultant and also worked with IBM for more than 10 years.

Lance Carlson has been programming Ruby since Rails version 0.13 was released, and he has been riding on its coattails since. He currently owns Ruby Skills, where he hacks with his team to develop web applications for small businesses and serial entrepreneurs. Lance has contributed to various Ruby open source projects such as Merb, Rails, and DataMapper, and he is also the creator of Ruby Anvil, an emerging desktop application framework. When Lance isn't hacking or running his business, you may find him playing soccer, riding his bike around Ann Arbor, or attending conferences.

Curt Hibbs has always been slightly obsessed with new technologies and tracking technology trends. But he will tell you that this is simply because he is lazy, always looking for new methods and technologies to make his work easier and more productive. This led to his discovery of Ruby in 2001 (when it was still relatively unknown outside of Japan), and to his founding several highly successful Ruby open source projects.

For most of his professional career, which started in the early 1970s, Curt has been a consultant to well-known companies such as Hewlett Packard, Intuit, Corel, WordStar, Charles Schwab, Vivendi Universal, and more. He has also been a principal in several startups. Curt now works as a senior software engineer for the Boeing Company in St. Louis.

Colophon

The animal on the cover of *Rails: Up and Running*, Second Edition, is an ibex (*Capra pyrenaica*). Found in the mountains of Europe, central Asia, and North Africa, the ibex spends most of its time at an altitude of 7,500 to 11,500 feet. The ibex is known for its impressively long horns, which can grow up to three feet on males. During mating season, ibex males bang their horns together in intense battles over mating rights.

Although the physics of such a feat seems dubious, according to legend, the ibex's horns were so strong that, if threatened, the animal could hurl itself from a precipice and land unharmed on them.

The cover image is from *Riverside Natural History*. The cover font is Adobe ITC Garamond. The text font is Linotype Birka; the heading font is Adobe Myriad Condensed; and the code font is LucasFont's TheSansMonoCondensed.

Related Titles from O'Reilly

Web Programming

ActionScript 3.0 Cookbook

ActionScript 3.0 Design Patterns

ActionScript for Flash MX: The Definitive Guide, *2nd Edition*

Advanced Rails

AIR for JavaScript Developer's Pocket Guide

Ajax Design Patterns

Ajax Hacks

Ajax on Rails

Ajax: The Definitive Guide

Building Scalable Web Sites

Designing Web Navigation

Dynamic HTML: The Definitive Reference, *3rd Edition*

Essential ActionScript 3.0

Essential PHP Security

Flash Hacks

Head First HTML with CSS & XHTML

Head Rush Ajax

High Performance Web Sites

HTTP: The Definitive Guide

JavaScript & DHTML Cookbook, *2nd Edition*

JavaScript Pocket Reference, *2nd Edition*

JavaScript: The Definitive Guide, *5th Edition*

Learning ActionScript 3.0

Learning PHP and MySQL, *2nd Edition*

PHP Cookbook, *2nd Edition*

PHP Hacks

PHP in a Nutshell

PHP Pocket Reference, *2nd Edition*

PHP Unit Pocket Guide

Programming ColdFusion MX, *2nd Edition*

Programming Flex 2

Programming PHP, *2nd Edition*

Programming Rails

Rails Cookbook

Upgrading to PHP 5

Web Database Applications with PHP and MySQL, *2nd Edition*

Web Scripting Power Tools

Web Site Cookbook

Webmaster in a Nutshell, *3rd Edition*

O'REILLY®

Our books are available at most retail and online bookstores.

To order direct: 1-800-998-9938 • *order@oreilly.com • www.oreilly.com*

Online editions of most O'Reilly titles are available by subscription at *safari.oreilly.com*

Try the online edition free for 45 days

Get the information you need when you need it, with Safari Books Online. Safari Books Online contains the complete version of the print book in your hands plus thousands of titles from the best technical publishers, with sample code ready to cut and paste into your applications.

Safari is designed for people in a hurry to get the answers they need so they can get the job done. You can find what you need in the morning, and put it to work in the afternoon. As simple as cut, paste, and program.

To try out Safari and the online edition of the above title FREE for 45 days, go to www.oreilly.com/go/safarienabled and enter the coupon code QGGKSAA.

To see the complete Safari Library visit:
safari.oreilly.com